The Thirty Ye

Volume 62

Friedrich Schiller

Alpha Editions

This edition published in 2023

ISBN : 9789357947619

Design and Setting By
Alpha Editions
www.alphaedis.com
Email - info@alphaedis.com

Contents

VOLUME 02

BOOK II.

The resolution which Ferdinand now adopted, gave to the war a new direction, a new scene, and new actors. From a rebellion in Bohemia, and the chastisement of rebels, a war extended first to Germany, and afterwards to Europe. It is, therefore, necessary to take a general survey of the state of affairs both in Germany and the rest of Europe.

Unequally as the territory of Germany and the privileges of its members were divided among the Roman Catholics and the Protestants, neither party could hope to maintain itself against the encroachments of its adversary otherwise than by a prudent use of its peculiar advantages, and by a politic union among themselves. If the Roman Catholics were the more numerous party, and more favoured by the constitution of the empire, the Protestants, on the other hand, had the advantage of possessing a more compact and populous line of territories, valiant princes, a warlike nobility, numerous armies, flourishing free towns, the command of the sea, and even at the worst, certainty of support from Roman Catholic states. If the Catholics could arm Spain and Italy in their favour, the republics of Venice, Holland, and England, opened their treasures to the Protestants, while the states of the North and the formidable power of Turkey, stood ready to afford them prompt assistance. Brandenburg, Saxony, and the Palatinate, opposed three Protestant to three Ecclesiastical votes in the Electoral College; while to the Elector of Bohemia, as to the Archduke of Austria, the possession of the Imperial dignity was an important check, if the Protestants properly availed themselves of it. The sword of the Union might keep within its sheath the sword of the League; or if matters actually came to a war, might make the issue of it doubtful. But, unfortunately, private interests dissolved the band of union which should have held together the Protestant members of the empire. This critical conjuncture found none but second-rate actors on the political stage, and the decisive moment was neglected because the courageous were deficient in power, and the powerful in sagacity, courage, and resolution.

The Elector of Saxony was placed at the head of the German Protestants, by the services of his ancestor Maurice, by the extent of his territories, and by the influence of his electoral vote. Upon the resolution he might adopt, the fate of the contending parties seemed to depend; and John George was not insensible to the advantages which this important situation procured him. Equally valuable as an ally, both to the Emperor and to the Protestant Union, he cautiously avoided committing himself to either party; neither trusting himself by any irrevocable declaration entirely to the gratitude of the Emperor, nor renouncing the advantages which were to be gained from his fears. Uninfected by the contagion of religious and romantic enthusiasm which hurried sovereign after sovereign to risk both crown and life on the hazard of war, John George aspired to the more solid renown of improving and advancing the interests of his territories. His cotemporaries accused him of forsaking the Protestant cause in the very midst of the storm; of preferring the aggrandizement of his house to the emancipation of his country; of exposing the whole Evangelical or Lutheran church of Germany to ruin, rather than raise an arm in defence of the Reformed or Calvinists; of injuring the common cause by his suspicious friendship more seriously than the open enmity of its avowed opponents. But it would have been well if his accusers had imitated the wise policy of the Elector. If, despite of the prudent policy, the Saxons, like all others, groaned at the cruelties which marked the Emperor's progress; if all Germany was a witness how Ferdinand deceived his confederates and trifled with his engagements; if even the Elector himself at last perceived this—the more shame to the Emperor who could so basely betray such implicit confidence.

If an excessive reliance on the Emperor, and the hope of enlarging his territories, tied the hands of the Elector of Saxony, the weak George William, Elector of Brandenburg, was still more shamefully fettered by fear of Austria, and of the loss of his dominions. What was made a reproach against these princes would have preserved to the Elector Palatine his fame and his kingdom. A rash confidence in his untried strength, the influence of French counsels, and the temptation of a crown, had seduced that unfortunate prince into an enterprise for which he had neither adequate genius nor political capacity. The partition of his territories among discordant princes, enfeebled the Palatinate, which, united, might have made a longer resistance.

This partition of territory was equally injurious to the House of Hesse, in which, between Darmstadt and Cassel, religious dissensions had occasioned a fatal division. The line of Darmstadt, adhering to the Confession of Augsburg, had placed itself under the Emperor's protection, who favoured it at the expense of the Calvinists of Cassel. While his religious confederates were shedding their blood for their faith and their liberties, the Landgrave of Darmstadt was won over by the Emperor's gold. But William of Cassel, every way worthy of his ancestor who, a century before, had defended the freedom of Germany against the formidable Charles V., espoused the cause of danger and of honour. Superior to that pusillanimity which made far more powerful princes bow before Ferdinand's might, the Landgrave William was the first to join the hero of Sweden, and to set an example to the princes of Germany which all had hesitated to begin. The boldness of his resolve was equalled by the steadfastness of his perseverance and the valour of his exploits. He placed himself with unshrinking resolution before his bleeding country, and boldly confronted the fearful enemy, whose hands were still reeking from the carnage of Magdeburg.

The Landgrave William deserves to descend to immortality with the heroic race of Ernest. Thy day of vengeance was long delayed, unfortunate John Frederick! Noble! never-to-be-forgotten prince! Slowly but brightly it broke. Thy times returned, and thy heroic spirit descended on thy grandson. An intrepid race of princes issues from the Thuringian forests, to shame, by immortal deeds, the unjust sentence which robbed thee of the electoral crown—to avenge thy offended shade by heaps of bloody sacrifice. The sentence of the conqueror could deprive thee of thy territories, but not that spirit of patriotism which staked them, nor that chivalrous courage which, a century afterwards, was destined to shake the throne of his descendant. Thy vengeance and that of Germany whetted the sacred sword, and one heroic hand after the other wielded the irresistible steel. As men, they achieved what as sovereigns they dared not undertake; they met in a glorious cause as the valiant soldiers of liberty. Too weak in territory to attack the enemy with their own forces, they directed foreign artillery against them, and led foreign banners to victory.

The liberties of Germany, abandoned by the more powerful states, who, however, enjoyed most of the prosperity accruing from them, were defended by a few princes for whom they were almost without value. The possession of territories and dignities deadened courage; the want of both made heroes. While Saxony, Brandenburg, and the rest drew back in terror, Anhalt, Mansfeld, the Prince of Weimar and others were shedding their blood in the field. The Dukes of Pomerania, Mecklenburg, Luneburg, and Wirtemberg, and the free cities of Upper Germany, to whom the name of EMPEROR was of course a formidable one, anxiously avoided a contest with such an opponent, and crouched murmuring beneath his mighty arm.

Austria and Roman Catholic Germany possessed in Maximilian of Bavaria a champion as prudent as he was powerful. Adhering throughout the war to one fixed plan, never divided between his religion and his political interests; not the slavish dependent of Austria, who was labouring for HIS advancement, and trembled before her powerful protector, Maximilian earned the territories and dignities that rewarded his exertions. The other Roman Catholic states, which were chiefly Ecclesiastical, too unwarlike to resist the multitudes whom the prosperity of their territories allured, became the victims of the war one after another, and were contented to persecute in the cabinet and in the pulpit, the enemy whom they could not openly oppose in the field. All of them, slaves either to Austria or Bavaria, sunk into insignificance by the side of Maximilian; in his hand alone their united power could be rendered available.

The formidable monarchy which Charles V. and his son had unnaturally constructed of the Netherlands, Milan, and the two Sicilies, and their distant possessions in the East and West Indies, was under Philip III. and Philip IV.

fast verging to decay. Swollen to a sudden greatness by unfruitful gold, this power was now sinking under a visible decline, neglecting, as it did, agriculture, the natural support of states. The conquests in the West Indies had reduced Spain itself to poverty, while they enriched the markets of Europe; the bankers of Antwerp, Venice, and Genoa, were making profit on the gold which was still buried in the mines of Peru. For the sake of India, Spain had been depopulated, while the treasures drawn from thence were wasted in the re-conquest of Holland, in the chimerical project of changing the succession to the crown of France, and in an unfortunate attack upon England. But the pride of this court had survived its greatness, as the hate of its enemies had outlived its power. Distrust of the Protestants suggested to the ministry of Philip III. the dangerous policy of his father; and the reliance of the Roman Catholics in Germany on Spanish assistance, was as firm as their belief in the wonder-working bones of the martyrs. External splendour concealed the inward wounds at which the life-blood of this monarchy was oozing; and the belief of its strength survived, because it still maintained the lofty tone of its golden days. Slaves in their palaces, and strangers even upon their own thrones, the Spanish nominal kings still gave laws to their German relations; though it is very doubtful if the support they afforded was worth the dependence by which the emperors purchased it. The fate of Europe was decided behind the Pyrenees by ignorant monks or vindictive favourites. Yet, even in its debasement, a power must always be formidable, which yields to none in extent; which, from custom, if not from the steadfastness of its views, adhered faithfully to one system of policy; which possessed well-disciplined armies and consummate generals; which, where the sword failed, did not scruple to employ the dagger; and converted even its ambassadors into incendiaries and assassins. What it had lost in three quarters of the globe, it now sought to regain to the eastward, and all Europe was at its mercy, if it could succeed in its long cherished design of uniting with the hereditary dominions of Austria all that lay between the Alps and the Adriatic.

To the great alarm of the native states, this formidable power had gained a footing in Italy, where its continual encroachments made the neighbouring sovereigns to tremble for their own possessions. The Pope himself was in the most dangerous situation; hemmed in on both sides by the Spanish Viceroys of Naples on the one side, and that of Milan upon the other. Venice was confined between the Austrian Tyrol and the Spanish territories in Milan. Savoy was surrounded by the latter and France. Hence the wavering and equivocal policy, which from the time of Charles V. had been pursued by the Italian States. The double character which pertained to the Popes made them perpetually vacillate between two contradictory systems of policy. If the successors of St. Peter found in the Spanish princes their most obedient disciples, and the most steadfast supporters of the Papal See, yet the princes of the States of the Church had in these monarchs their most dangerous neighbours, and most formidable opponents. If, in the one capacity, their dearest wish was the destruction of the Protestants, and the triumph of Austria, in the other, they had reason to bless the arms of the Protestants, which disabled a dangerous enemy. The one or the other sentiment prevailed, according as the love of temporal dominion, or zeal for spiritual supremacy, predominated in the mind of the Pope. But the policy of Rome was, on the whole, directed to immediate dangers; and it is well known how far more powerful is the apprehension of losing a present good, than anxiety to recover a long lost possession. And thus it becomes intelligible how the Pope should first combine with Austria for the destruction of heresy, and then conspire with these very heretics for the destruction of Austria. Strangely blended are the threads of human affairs! What would have become of the Reformation, and of the liberties of Germany, if the Bishop of Rome and the Prince of Rome had had but one interest?

France had lost with its great Henry all its importance and all its weight in the political balance of Europe. A turbulent minority had destroyed all the benefits of the able administration of Henry. Incapable ministers, the creatures of court intrigue, squandered in a few years the treasures which Sully's economy and Henry's frugality had amassed. Scarce able to maintain their ground against internal factions, they were compelled to resign to other hands the helm of European affairs. The same civil war which armed Germany against itself, excited a similar commotion in France; and Louis XIII. attained majority only to wage a war with his own mother and his Protestant subjects. This party, which had been kept quiet by Henry's enlightened policy, now seized the opportunity to take up arms, and, under the command of some adventurous leaders, began to form themselves into a party within the state, and to fix on the strong and powerful town of Rochelle as the capital of their intended kingdom. Too little of a statesman to suppress, by a prudent toleration, this civil commotion in its birth, and too little master of the resources of his kingdom to direct them with energy, Louis XIII. was reduced to the degradation of purchasing the submission of the rebels by large sums of money. Though policy might incline him, in one point of view, to assist the Bohemian insurgents against Austria, the son of Henry the Fourth was now compelled to be an inactive spectator of their destruction, happy enough if the Calvinists in his own dominions did not unseasonably bethink them of their confederates beyond the Rhine. A great mind at the helm of state would have reduced the Protestants in France to obedience, while it employed them to fight for the independence of their German brethren. But Henry IV. was no more, and Richelieu had not yet revived his system of policy.

While the glory of France was thus upon the wane, the emancipated republic of Holland was completing the fabric of its greatness. The enthusiastic courage had not yet died away which, enkindled by the House of Orange, had converted this mercantile people into a nation of heroes, and had enabled them to maintain their independence in a bloody war against the Spanish monarchy. Aware how much they owed their own liberty to foreign support, these republicans were ready to assist their German brethren in a similar cause, and the more so, as both were opposed to the same enemy, and the liberty of Germany was the best warrant for that of Holland. But a republic which had still to battle for its very existence, which, with all its wonderful exertions, was scarce a match for the formidable enemy within its own territories, could not be expected to withdraw its troops from the necessary work of self-defence to employ them with a magnanimous policy in protecting foreign states.

England too, though now united with Scotland, no longer possessed, under the weak James, that influence in the affairs of Europe which the governing mind of Elizabeth had procured for it. Convinced that the welfare of her dominions depended on the security of the Protestants, this politic princess had never swerved from the principle of promoting every enterprise which had for its object the diminution of the Austrian power. Her successor was no less devoid of capacity to comprehend, than of vigour to execute, her views. While the economical Elizabeth spared not her treasures to support the Flemings against Spain, and Henry IV. against the League, James abandoned his daughter, his son-in-law, and his grandchild, to the fury of their enemies. While he exhausted his learning to establish the divine right of kings, he allowed his own dignity to sink into the dust; while he exerted his rhetoric to prove the absolute authority of kings, he reminded the people of theirs; and by a useless profusion, sacrificed the chief of his sovereign rights— that of dispensing with his parliament, and thus depriving liberty of its organ. An innate horror at the sight of a naked sword averted him from the most just of wars; while his favourite Buckingham practised on his weakness, and his own complacent vanity rendered him an easy dupe of Spanish artifice. While his son-in-law was ruined, and the inheritance of his grandson given to others, this weak prince was imbibing, with satisfaction, the incense which was offered to him by Austria and Spain. To divert his attention from the German war, he was amused with the proposal of a Spanish marriage for his son, and the ridiculous parent encouraged the romantic youth in the foolish project of paying his addresses in person to the Spanish princess. But his son lost his bride, as his son-in-law lost the crown of Bohemia and the Palatine Electorate; and death alone saved him from the danger of closing his pacific reign by a war at home, which he never had courage to maintain, even at a distance.

The domestic disturbances which his misgovernment had gradually excited burst forth under his unfortunate son, and forced him, after some unimportant attempts, to renounce all further participation in the German war, in order to stem within his own kingdom the rage of faction.

Two illustrious monarchs, far unequal in personal reputation, but equal in power and desire of fame, made the North at this time to be respected. Under the long and active reign of Christian IV., Denmark had risen into importance. The personal qualifications of this prince, an excellent navy, a formidable army, well-ordered finances, and prudent alliances, had combined to give her prosperity at home and influence abroad. Gustavus Vasa had rescued Sweden from vassalage, reformed it by wise laws, and had introduced, for the first time, this newly-organized state into the field of European politics. What this great prince had merely sketched in rude outline, was filled up by Gustavus Adolphus, his still greater grandson.

These two kingdoms, once unnaturally united and enfeebled by their union, had been violently separated at the time of the Reformation, and this separation was the epoch of their prosperity. Injurious as this compulsory union had proved to both kingdoms, equally necessary to each apart were neighbourly friendship and harmony. On both the evangelical church leaned; both had the same seas to protect; a common interest ought to unite them against the same enemy. But the hatred which had dissolved the union of these monarchies continued long after their separation to divide the two nations. The Danish kings could not abandon their pretensions to the Swedish crown, nor the Swedes banish the remembrance of Danish oppression. The contiguous boundaries of the two kingdoms constantly furnished materials for international quarrels, while the watchful jealousy of both kings, and the unavoidable collision of their commercial interests in the North Seas, were inexhaustible sources of dispute.

Among the means of which Gustavus Vasa, the founder of the Swedish monarchy, availed himself to strengthen his new edifice, the Reformation had been one of the principal. A fundamental law of the kingdom excluded the adherents of popery from all offices of the state, and prohibited every future sovereign of Sweden from altering the religious constitution of the kingdom. But the second son and second successor of Gustavus had relapsed into popery, and his son Sigismund, also king of Poland, had been guilty of measures which menaced both the constitution and the established church. Headed by Charles, Duke of Sudermania, the third son of Gustavus, the Estates made a courageous resistance, which terminated, at last, in an open civil war between the uncle and nephew, and between the King and the people. Duke Charles, administrator of the kingdom during the absence of the king, had availed himself of Sigismund's long residence in Poland, and the just displeasure of the states, to ingratiate himself with the nation, and gradually to prepare his way to the throne. His views were not a little forwarded by Sigismund's imprudence. A general Diet ventured to abolish, in favour of the Protector, the rule of primogeniture which Gustavus had established in the succession, and placed the Duke of Sudermania on the throne, from which Sigismund, with his whole posterity, were solemnly excluded. The son of the new king (who reigned under the name of Charles IX.) was Gustavus Adolphus, whom, as the son of a usurper, the adherents of Sigismund refused to recognize. But if the obligations between monarchy and subjects are reciprocal, and states are not to be transmitted, like a lifeless heirloom, from hand to hand, a nation acting with unanimity must have the power of renouncing their allegiance to a sovereign who has violated his obligations to them, and of filling his place by a worthier object.

Gustavus Adolphus had not completed his seventeenth year, when the Swedish throne became vacant by the death of his father. But the early maturity of his genius enabled the Estates to abridge in his favour the legal period of minority. With a glorious conquest over himself he commenced a reign which was to have victory for its constant attendant, a career which was to begin and end in success. The young Countess of Brahe, the daughter of a subject, had gained his early affections, and he had resolved to share with her the Swedish throne. But, constrained by time and circumstances, he made his attachment yield to the higher duties of a king, and heroism again took exclusive possession of a heart which was not destined by nature to confine itself within the limits of quiet domestic happiness.

Christian IV. of Denmark, who had ascended the throne before the birth of Gustavus, in an inroad upon Sweden, had gained some considerable advantages over the father of that hero. Gustavus Adolphus hastened to put an end to this destructive war, and by prudent sacrifices obtained a peace, in order to turn his arms against the Czar of Muscovy. The questionable fame of a conqueror never tempted him to spend the blood of his subjects in unjust wars; but he never shrunk from a just one. His arms were successful against Russia, and Sweden was augmented by several important provinces on the east.

In the meantime, Sigismund of Poland retained against the son the same sentiments of hostility which the father had provoked, and left no artifice untried to shake the allegiance of his subjects, to cool the ardour of his friends, and to embitter his enemies. Neither the great qualities of his rival, nor the repeated proofs of devotion which Sweden gave to her loved monarch, could extinguish in this infatuated prince the foolish hope of regaining his lost throne. All Gustavus's overtures were haughtily rejected. Unwillingly was this really peaceful king involved in a tedious war with Poland, in which the whole of Livonia and Polish Prussia were successively conquered. Though constantly victorious, Gustavus Adolphus was always the first to hold out the hand of peace.

This contest between Sweden and Poland falls somewhere about the beginning of the Thirty Years' War in Germany, with which it is in some measure connected. It was enough that Sigismund, himself a Roman Catholic, was disputing the Swedish crown with a Protestant prince, to assure him the active support of Spain and Austria; while a double relationship to the Emperor gave him a still stronger claim to his protection. It was his reliance on this powerful assistance that chiefly encouraged the King of Poland to continue the war, which had hitherto turned out so unfavourably for him, and the courts of Madrid and Vienna failed not to encourage him by high-sounding promises. While Sigismund lost one place after another in Livonia, Courland, and Prussia, he saw his ally in Germany advancing from conquest after conquest to unlimited power. No wonder then if his aversion to peace kept pace with his losses. The vehemence with which he nourished his chimerical hopes blinded him to the artful policy of his confederates, who at his expense were keeping the Swedish hero employed, in order to overturn, without opposition, the liberties of Germany, and then to seize on the exhausted North as an easy conquest. One circumstance which had not been calculated on—the magnanimity of Gustavus— overthrew this deceitful policy. An eight years' war in Poland, so far from exhausting the power of Sweden, had only served to mature the military genius of Gustavus, to inure the Swedish army to warfare, and insensibly to perfect that system of tactics by which they were afterwards to perform such wonders in Germany.

After this necessary digression on the existing circumstances of Europe, I now resume the thread of my history.

Ferdinand had regained his dominions, but had not indemnified himself for the expenses of recovering them. A sum of forty millions of florins, which the confiscations in Bohemia and Moravia had produced, would have sufficed to reimburse both himself and his allies; but the Jesuits and his favourites soon squandered this sum, large as it was. Maximilian, Duke of Bavaria, to whose victorious arm, principally, the Emperor owed the recovery of his dominions; who, in the service of religion and the Emperor, had sacrificed his near relation, had the strongest claims on his gratitude; and moreover, in a treaty which, before the war, the duke had concluded with the Emperor, he had expressly stipulated for the reimbursement of all expenses. Ferdinand felt the full weight of the obligation imposed upon him by this treaty and by these services, but he was not disposed to discharge it at his own cost. His purpose was to bestow a brilliant reward upon the duke, but without detriment to himself. How could this be done better than at the expense of the unfortunate prince who, by his revolt, had given the Emperor a right to punish him, and whose offences might be painted in colours strong enough to justify the most violent measures under the appearance of law. That, then, Maximilian may be rewarded, Frederick must be further persecuted and totally ruined; and to defray the expenses of the old war, a new one must be commenced.

But a still stronger motive combined to enforce the first. Hitherto Ferdinand had been contending for existence alone; he had been fulfilling no other duty than that of self-defence. But now, when victory gave him freedom to act, a higher duty occurred to him, and he remembered the vow which he had made at Loretto and at Rome, to his generalissima, the Holy Virgin, to extend her worship even at the risk of his crown and life. With this object, the oppression of the Protestants was inseparably connected. More favourable circumstances for its accomplishment could not offer than those which presented themselves at the close of the Bohemian war. Neither the power, nor a pretext of right, were now wanting to enable him to place the Palatinate in the hands of the Catholics, and the importance of this change to the Catholic interests in Germany would be incalculable. Thus, in rewarding the Duke of Bavaria with the spoils of his relation, he at once gratified his meanest passions and fulfilled his most exalted duties; he crushed an enemy whom he hated, and spared his avarice a painful sacrifice, while he believed he was winning a heavenly crown.

In the Emperor's cabinet, the ruin of Frederick had been resolved upon long before fortune had decided against him; but it was only after this event that they ventured to direct against him the thunders of arbitrary power. A decree of the Emperor, destitute of all the formalities required on such occasions by the laws of the Empire, pronounced the Elector, and three other princes who had borne arms for him at Silesia and Bohemia, as offenders against the imperial majesty, and disturbers of the public peace, under the ban of the empire, and deprived them of their titles and territories. The execution of this sentence against Frederick, namely the seizure of his lands, was, in further contempt of law, committed to Spain as Sovereign of the circle of Burgundy, to the Duke of Bavaria, and the League. Had the Evangelic Union been worthy of the name it bore, and of the cause which it pretended to defend, insuperable obstacles might have prevented the execution of the sentence; but it was hopeless for a power which was far from a match even for the Spanish troops in the Lower Palatinate, to contend against the united strength of the Emperor, Bavaria, and the League. The sentence of proscription pronounced upon the Elector soon detached the free cities from the Union; and the princes quickly followed their example. Fortunate in preserving their own dominions, they abandoned the Elector, their former chief, to the Emperor's mercy, renounced the Union, and vowed never to revive it again.

But while thus ingloriously the German princes deserted the unfortunate Frederick, and while Bohemia, Silesia, and Moravia submitted to the Emperor, a single man, a soldier of fortune, whose only treasure was his sword, Ernest Count Mansfeld, dared, in the Bohemian town of Pilsen, to defy the whole power of Austria. Left without assistance after the battle of Prague by the Elector, to whose service he had devoted himself, and even uncertain whether Frederick would thank him for his perseverance, he alone for some time held out against the imperialists, till the garrison, mutinying for want of pay, sold the town to the Emperor. Undismayed by this reverse, he immediately commenced new levies in the Upper Palatinate, and enlisted the disbanded troops of the Union. A new army of 20,000 men was soon assembled under his banners, the more formidable to the provinces which might be the object of its attack, because it must subsist by plunder. Uncertain where this swarm might light, the neighbouring bishops trembled for their rich possessions, which offered a tempting prey to its ravages. But, pressed by the Duke of Bavaria, who now entered the Upper Palatinate, Mansfeld was compelled to retire. Eluding, by a successful stratagem, the Bavarian general, Tilly, who was in pursuit of him, he suddenly appeared in the Lower Palatinate, and there wreaked upon the bishoprics of the Rhine the severities he had designed for those of Franconia. While the imperial and Bavarian allies thus overran Bohemia, the Spanish general, Spinola, had penetrated with a numerous army from the Netherlands into the Lower Palatinate, which, however, the pacification of Ulm permitted the Union to defend. But their measures were so badly concerted, that one place after another fell into the hands of the Spaniards; and at last, when the Union broke up, the greater part of the country was in the possession of Spain. The Spanish general, Corduba, who commanded these troops after the recall of Spinola, hastily raised the siege of Frankenthal, when Mansfeld entered the Lower Palatinate. But instead of driving the Spaniards out of this province, he hastened across the Rhine to secure for his needy troops shelter and subsistence in Alsace. The open countries on which this swarm of maurauders threw themselves were converted into frightful deserts, and only by enormous contributions could the cities purchase an exemption from plunder. Reinforced by this expedition, Mansfeld again appeared on the Rhine to cover the Lower Palatinate.

So long as such an arm fought for him, the cause of the Elector Frederick was not·irretrievably lost. New prospects began to open, and misfortune raised up friends who had been silent during his prosperity. King James of England, who had looked on with indifference while his son-in-law lost the Bohemian crown, was aroused from his insensibility when the very existence of his daughter and grandson was at stake, and the victorious enemy ventured an attack upon the Electorate. Late enough, he at last opened his treasures, and hastened to afford supplies of money and troops, first to the Union, which at that time was defending the Lower Palatinate, and afterwards, when they retired, to Count Mansfeld. By his means his near relation, Christian, King of Denmark, was induced to afford his active support. At the same time, the approaching expiration of the truce between Spain and Holland deprived the Emperor of all the supplies which otherwise he might expect from the side of the Netherlands. More important still was the assistance which the Palatinate received from Transylvania and Hungary. The cessation of hostilities between Gabor and the Emperor was scarcely at an end, when this old and formidable enemy of Austria overran Hungary anew, and caused himself to be crowned king in Presburg. So rapid was his progress that, to protect Austria and Hungary, Boucquoi was obliged to evacuate Bohemia. This brave general met his death at the siege of Neuhausel, as, shortly before, the no less valiant Dampierre had fallen before Presburg. Gabor's march into the Austrian territory was irresistible; the old Count Thurn, and several other distinguished Bohemians, had united their hatred and their strength with this irreconcileable enemy of Austria. A vigorous attack on the side of Germany, while Gabor pressed the Emperor on that of Hungary, might have retrieved the fortunes of Frederick; but, unfortunately, the Bohemians and Germans had always laid down their arms when Gabor took the field; and the latter was always exhausted at the very moment that the former began to recover their vigour.

Meanwhile Frederick had not delayed to join his protector Mansfeld. In disguise he entered the Lower Palatinate, of which the possession was at that time disputed between Mansfeld and the Bavarian general, Tilly, the Upper Palatinate having been long conquered. A ray of hope shone upon him as, from the wreck of the Union, new friends came forward. A former member of the Union, George Frederick, Margrave of Baden, had for some time been engaged in assembling a military force, which soon amounted to a considerable army. Its destination was kept a secret till he suddenly took the field and joined Mansfeld. Before commencing the war, he resigned his Margraviate to his son, in the hope of eluding, by this precaution, the Emperor's revenge, if his enterprize should be unsuccessful. His neighbour, the Duke of Wirtemberg, likewise began to augment his military force. The courage of the Palatine revived, and he laboured assiduously to renew the Protestant Union. It was now time for Tilly to consult for his own safety, and he hastily summoned the Spanish troops, under Corduba, to his assistance. But while the enemy was uniting his strength, Mansfeld and the Margrave separated, and the latter was defeated by the Bavarian general near Wimpfen (1622).

To defend a king whom his nearest relation persecuted, and who was deserted even by his own father-in-law, there had come forward an adventurer without money, and whose very legitimacy was questioned. A sovereign had resigned possessions over which he reigned in peace, to hazard the uncertain fortune of war in behalf of a stranger. And now another soldier of fortune, poor in territorial possessions, but rich in illustrious ancestry, undertook the defence of a cause which the former despaired of. Christian, Duke of Brunswick, administrator of Halberstadt, seemed to have learnt from Count Mansfeld the secret of keeping in the field an army of 20,000 men without money. Impelled by youthful presumption, and influenced partly by the wish of establishing his reputation at the expense of the Roman Catholic priesthood, whom he cordially detested, and partly by a thirst for plunder, he assembled a considerable army in Lower Saxony, under the pretext of espousing the defence of Frederick, and of the liberties of Germany. "God's Friend, Priest's Foe", was the motto he chose for his coinage, which was struck out of church plate; and his conduct belied one half at least of the device.

The progress of these banditti was, as usual, marked by the most frightful devastation. Enriched by the spoils of the chapters of Lower Saxony and Westphalia, they gathered strength to plunder the bishoprics upon the Upper Rhine. Driven from thence, both by friends and foes, the Administrator approached the town of Hoechst on the Maine, which he crossed after a murderous action with Tilly, who disputed with him the passage of the river. With the loss of half his army he reached the opposite bank, where he quickly collected his shattered troops, and formed a junction with Mansfeld. Pursued by Tilly, this united host threw itself again into Alsace, to repeat their former ravages. While the Elector Frederick followed, almost like a fugitive mendicant, this swarm of plunderers which acknowledged him as its lord, and dignified itself with his name, his friends were busily endeavouring to effect a reconciliation between him and the Emperor. Ferdinand took care not to deprive them of all hope of seeing the Palatine restored to his dominion. Full of artifice and dissimulation, he pretended to be willing to enter into a negotiation, hoping thereby to cool their ardour in the field, and to prevent them from driving matters to extremity. James I., ever the dupe of Spanish cunning, contributed not a little, by his foolish intermeddling, to promote the Emperor's schemes. Ferdinand insisted that Frederick, if he would appeal to his clemency, should, first of all, lay down his arms, and James considered this demand extremely reasonable. At his instigation, the Elector dismissed his only real defenders, Count Mansfeld and the Administrator, and in Holland awaited his own fate from the mercy of the Emperor.

Mansfeld and Duke Christian were now at a loss for some new name; the cause of the Elector had not set them in motion, so his dismissal could not disarm them. War was their object; it was all the same to them in whose cause or name it was waged. After some vain attempts on the part of Mansfeld to be received into the Emperor's service, both marched into Lorraine, where the excesses of their troops spread terror even to the heart of France. Here they long waited in vain for a master willing to purchase their services; till the

Dutch, pressed by the Spanish General Spinola, offered to take them into pay. After a bloody fight at Fleurus with the Spaniards, who attempted to intercept them, they reached Holland, where their appearance compelled the Spanish general forthwith to raise the siege of Bergen-op-Zoom. But even Holland was soon weary of these dangerous guests, and availed herself of the first moment to get rid of their unwelcome assistance. Mansfeld allowed his troops to recruit themselves for new enterprises in the fertile province of East Friezeland. Duke Christian, passionately enamoured of the Electress Palatine, with whom he had become acquainted in Holland, and more disposed for war than ever, led back his army into Lower Saxony, bearing that princess's glove in his hat, and on his standards the motto "All for God and Her". Neither of these adventurers had as yet run their career in this war.

All the imperial territories were now free from the enemy; the Union was dissolved; the Margrave of Baden, Duke Christian, and Mansfeld, driven from the field, and the Palatinate overrun by the executive troops of the empire. Manheim and Heidelberg were in possession of Bavaria, and Frankenthal was shortly afterwards ceded to the Spaniards. The Palatine, in a distant corner of Holland, awaited the disgraceful permission to appease, by abject submission, the vengeance of the Emperor; and an Electoral Diet was at last summoned to decide his fate. That fate, however, had been long before decided at the court of the Emperor; though now, for the first time, were circumstances favourable for giving publicity to the decision. After his past measures towards the Elector, Ferdinand believed that a sincere reconciliation was not to be hoped for. The violent course he had once begun, must be completed successfully, or recoil upon himself. What was already lost was irrecoverable; Frederick could never hope to regain his dominions; and a prince without territory and without subjects had little chance of retaining the electoral crown. Deeply as the Palatine had offended against the House of Austria, the services of the Duke of Bavaria were no less meritorious. If the House of Austria and the Roman Catholic church had much to dread from the resentment and religious rancour of the Palatine family, they had as much to hope from the gratitude and religious zeal of the Bavarian. Lastly, by the cession of the Palatine Electorate to Bavaria, the Roman Catholic religion would obtain a decisive preponderance in the Electoral College, and secure a permanent triumph in Germany.

The last circumstance was sufficient to win the support of the three Ecclesiastical Electors to this innovation; and among the Protestants the vote of Saxony was alone of any importance. But could John George be expected to dispute with the Emperor a right, without which he would expose to question his own title to the electoral dignity? To a prince whom descent, dignity, and political power placed at the head of the Protestant church in Germany, nothing, it is true, ought to be more sacred than the defence of the rights of that church against all the encroachments of the Roman Catholics. But the question here was not whether the interests of the Protestants were to be supported against the Roman Catholics, but which of two religions equally detested, the Calvinistic and the Popish, was to triumph over the other; to which of the two enemies, equally dangerous, the Palatinate was to be assigned; and in this clashing of opposite duties, it was natural that private hate and private gain should determine the event. The born protector of the liberties of Germany, and of the Protestant religion, encouraged the Emperor to dispose of the Palatinate by his imperial prerogative; and to apprehend no resistance on the part of Saxony to his measures on the mere ground of form. If the Elector was afterwards disposed to retract this consent, Ferdinand himself, by driving the Evangelical preachers from Bohemia, was the cause of this change of opinion; and, in the eyes of the Elector, the transference of the Palatine Electorate to Bavaria ceased to be illegal, as soon as Ferdinand was prevailed upon to cede Lusatia to Saxony, in consideration of six millions of dollars, as the expenses of the war.

Thus, in defiance of all Protestant Germany, and in mockery of the fundamental laws of the empire, which, as his election, he had sworn to maintain, Ferdinand at Ratisbon solemnly invested the Duke of Bavaria with the Palatinate, without prejudice, as the form ran, to the rights which the relations or descendants of Frederick might afterwards establish. That unfortunate prince thus saw himself irrevocably driven from his possessions, without having been even heard before the tribunal which condemned him— a privilege which the law allows to the meanest subject, and even to the most atrocious criminal.

This violent step at last opened the eyes of the King of England; and as the negociations for the marriage of his son with the Infanta of Spain were now broken off, James began seriously to espouse the cause of his son-in-law. A change in the French ministry had placed Cardinal Richelieu at the head of affairs, and this fallen kingdom soon began to feel that a great mind was at the helm of state. The attempts of the Spanish Viceroy in Milan to gain possession of the Valtelline, and thus to form a junction with the Austrian hereditary dominions, revived the olden dread of this power, and with it the policy of Henry the Great. The marriage of the Prince of Wales with Henrietta of France, established a close union between the two crowns; and to this alliance, Holland, Denmark, and some of the Italian states presently acceded. Its object was to expel, by force of arms, Spain from the Valtelline, and to compel Austria to reinstate Frederick; but only the first of these designs was prosecuted with vigour. James I. died, and Charles I., involved in disputes with his Parliament, could not bestow attention on the affairs of Germany. Savoy and Venice withheld their assistance; and the French minister thought it necessary to subdue the Huguenots at home, before he supported the German Protestants against the Emperor. Great as were the hopes which had been formed from this alliance, they were yet equalled by the disappointment of the event.

Mansfeld, deprived of all support, remained inactive on the Lower Rhine; and Duke Christian of Brunswick, after an unsuccessful campaign, was a second time driven out of Germany. A fresh irruption of Bethlen Gabor into Moravia, frustrated by the want of support from the Germans, terminated, like all the rest, in a formal peace with the Emperor. The Union was no more; no Protestant prince was in arms; and on the frontiers of Lower Germany, the Bavarian General Tilly, at the head of a victorious army, encamped in the Protestant territory. The movements of the Duke of Brunswick had drawn him into this quarter, and even into the circle of Lower Saxony, when he made himself master of the Administrator's magazines at Lippstadt. The necessity of observing this enemy, and preventing him from new inroads, was the pretext assigned for continuing Tilly's stay in the country. But, in truth, both Mansfeld and Duke Christian had, from want of money, disbanded their armies, and Count Tilly had no enemy to dread. Why, then, still burden the country with his presence?

It is difficult, amidst the uproar of contending parties, to distinguish the voice of truth; but certainly it was matter for alarm that the League did not lay down its arms. The premature rejoicings of the Roman Catholics, too, were calculated to increase apprehension. The Emperor and the League stood armed and victorious in Germany without a power to oppose them, should they venture to attack the Protestant states and to annul the religious treaty. Had Ferdinand been in reality far from disposed to abuse his conquests, still the defenceless position of the Protestants was most likely to suggest the temptation. Obsolete conventions could not bind a prince who thought that he owed all to religion, and believed that a religious creed would sanctify any deed, however violent. Upper Germany was already overpowered. Lower Germany alone could check his despotic authority. Here the Protestants still predominated; the church had been forcibly deprived of most of its endowments; and the present appeared a favourable moment for recovering these lost possessions. A great part of the strength of the Lower German princes consisted in these Chapters, and the plea of restoring its own to the church, afforded an excellent pretext for weakening these princes.

Unpardonable would have been their negligence, had they remained inactive in this danger. The remembrance of the ravages which Tilly's army had committed in Lower Saxony was too recent not to arouse the Estates to measures of defence. With all haste, the circle of Lower Saxony began to arm itself. Extraordinary contributions were levied, troops collected, and magazines filled. Negociations for subsidies were set on foot with Venice, Holland, and England. They deliberated, too, what power should be placed at the head of the confederacy. The kings of the Sound and the Baltic, the natural allies of this circle, would not see with indifference the Emperor treating it as a conqueror, and establishing himself as their neighbour on the shores of the North Sea. The twofold interests of religion and policy urged them to put a stop to his progress in Lower Germany. Christian IV. of Denmark, as Duke of Holstein, was himself a prince of this circle, and by considerations equally powerful, Gustavus Adolphus of Sweden was induced to join the confederacy.

These two kings vied with each other for the honour of defending Lower Saxony, and of opposing the formidable power of Austria. Each offered to raise a well-disciplined army, and to lead it in person. His victorious campaigns against Moscow and Poland gave weight to the promises of the King of Sweden. The shores of the Baltic were full of the name of Gustavus. But the fame of his rival excited the envy of the Danish monarch; and the more success he promised himself in this campaign, the less disposed was he to show any favour to his envied neighbour. Both laid their conditions and plans before the English ministry, and Christian IV. finally succeeded in outbidding his rival. Gustavus Adolphus, for his own security, had demanded the cession of some places of strength in Germany, where he himself had no territories, to afford, in case of need, a place of refuge for his troops. Christian IV. possessed Holstein and Jutland, through which, in the event of a defeat, he could always secure a retreat.

Eager to get the start of his competitor, the King of Denmark hastened to take the field. Appointed generalissimo of the circle of Lower Saxony, he soon had an army of 60,000 men in motion; the administrator of Magdeburg, and the Dukes of Brunswick and Mecklenburgh, entered into an alliance with him. Encouraged by the hope of assistance from England, and the possession of so large a force, he flattered himself he should be able to terminate the war in a single campaign.

At Vienna, it was officially notified that the only object of these preparations was the protection of the circle, and the maintenance of peace. But the negociations with Holland, England, and even France, the extraordinary exertions of the circle, and the raising of so formidable an army, seemed to have something more in view than defensive operations, and to contemplate nothing less than the complete restoration of the Elector Palatine, and the humiliation of the dreaded power of Austria.

After negociations, exhortations, commands, and threats had in vain been employed by the Emperor in order to induce the King of Denmark and the circle of Lower Saxony to lay down their arms, hostilities commenced, and Lower Germany became the theatre of war. Count Tilly, marching along the left bank of the Weser, made himself master of all the passes as far as Minden.

After an unsuccessful attack on Nieuburg, he crossed the river and overran the principality of Calemberg, in which he quartered his troops. The king conducted his operations on the right bank of the river, and spread his forces over the territories of Brunswick, but having weakened his main body by too powerful detachments, he could not engage in any enterprise of importance. Aware of his opponent's superiority, he avoided a decisive action as anxiously as the general of the League sought it.

With the exception of the troops from the Spanish Netherlands, which had poured into the Lower Palatinate, the Emperor had hitherto made use only of the arms of Bavaria and the League in Germany. Maximilian conducted the war as executor of the ban of the empire, and Tilly, who commanded the army of execution, was in the Bavarian service. The Emperor owed superiority in the field to Bavaria and the League, and his fortunes were in their hands. This dependence on their goodwill, but ill accorded with the grand schemes, which the brilliant commencement of the war had led the imperial cabinet to form.

However active the League had shown itself in the Emperor's defence, while thereby it secured its own welfare, it could not be expected that it would enter as readily into his views of conquest. Or, if they still continued to lend their armies for that purpose, it was too much to be feared that they would share with the Emperor nothing but general odium, while they appropriated to themselves all advantages. A strong army under his own orders could alone free him from this debasing dependence upon Bavaria, and restore to him his former pre-eminence in Germany. But the war had already exhausted the imperial dominions, and they were unequal to the expense of such an armament. In these circumstances, nothing could be more welcome to the Emperor than the proposal with which one of his officers surprised him.

This was Count Wallenstein, an experienced officer, and the richest nobleman in Bohemia. From his earliest youth he had been in the service of the House of Austria, and several campaigns against the Turks, Venetians, Bohemians, Hungarians, and Transylvanians had established his reputation. He was present as colonel at the battle of Prague, and afterwards, as major-general, had defeated a Hungarian force in Moravia. The Emperor's gratitude was equal to his services, and a large share of the confiscated estates of the Bohemian insurgents was their reward. Possessed of immense property, excited by ambitious views, confident in his own good fortune, and still more encouraged by the existing state of circumstances, he offered, at his own expense and that of his friends, to raise and clothe an army for the Emperor, and even undertook the cost of maintaining it, if he were allowed to augment it to 50,000 men. The project was universally ridiculed as the chimerical offspring of a visionary brain; but the offer was highly valuable, if its promises should be but partially fulfilled. Certain circles in Bohemia were assigned to him as depots, with authority to appoint his own officers. In a few months he had 20,000 men under arms, with which, quitting the Austrian territories, he soon afterwards appeared on the frontiers of Lower Saxony with 30,000. The Emperor had lent this armament nothing but his name. The reputation of the general, the prospect of rapid promotion, and the hope of plunder, attracted to his standard adventurers from all quarters of Germany; and even sovereign princes, stimulated by the desire of glory or of gain, offered to raise regiments for the service of Austria.

Now, therefore, for the first time in this war, an imperial army appeared in Germany;—an event which if it was menacing to the Protestants, was scarcely more acceptable to the Catholics. Wallenstein had orders to unite his army with the troops of the League, and in conjunction with the Bavarian general to attack the King of Denmark. But long jealous of Tilly's fame, he showed no disposition to share with him the laurels of the campaign, or in the splendour of his rival's achievements to dim the lustre of his own. His plan of operations was to support the latter, but to act entirely independent of him. As he had not resources, like Tilly, for supplying the wants of his army, he was obliged to march his troops into fertile countries which had not as yet suffered from war. Disobeying, therefore, the order to form a junction with the general of the League, he marched into the territories of Halberstadt and Magdeburg, and at Dessau made himself master of the Elbe. All the lands on either bank of this river were at his command, and from them he could either attack the King of Denmark in the rear, or, if prudent, enter the territories of that prince.

Christian IV. was fully aware of the danger of his situation between two such powerful armies. He had already been joined by the administrator of Halberstadt, who had lately returned from Holland; he now also acknowledged Mansfeld, whom previously he had refused to recognise, and supported him to the best of his ability. Mansfeld amply requited this service. He alone kept at bay the army of Wallenstein upon the Elbe, and prevented its junction with that of Tilly, and a combined attack on the King of Denmark. Notwithstanding the enemy's superiority, this intrepid general even approached the bridge of Dessau, and ventured to entrench himself in presence of the imperial lines. But attacked in the rear by the whole force of the Imperialists, he was obliged to yield to superior numbers, and to abandon his post with the loss of 3,000 killed. After this defeat, Mansfeld withdrew into Brandenburg, where he soon recruited and reinforced his army; and suddenly turned into Silesia, with the view of marching from thence into Hungary; and, in conjunction with Bethlen Gabor, carrying the war into the heart of Austria. As the Austrian dominions in that quarter were entirely defenceless, Wallenstein received immediate orders to leave the King of Denmark, and if possible to intercept Mansfeld's progress through Silesia.

The diversion which this movement of Mansfeld had made in the plans of Wallenstein, enabled the king to detach a part of his force into Westphalia, to seize the bishoprics of Munster and Osnaburg. To check this movement, Tilly suddenly moved from the Weser; but the operations of Duke Christian, who threatened the territories of the League with an inroad in the direction of Hesse, and to remove thither the seat of war, recalled him as rapidly from Westphalia. In order to keep open his communication with these provinces, and to prevent the junction of the enemy with the Landgrave of Hesse, Tilly hastily seized all the tenable posts on the Werha and Fulda, and took up a strong position in Minden, at the foot of the Hessian Mountains, and at the confluence of these rivers with the Weser. He soon made himself master of Goettingen, the key of Brunswick and Hesse, and was meditating a similar attack upon Nordheim, when the king advanced upon him with his whole army. After throwing into this place the necessary supplies for a long siege, the latter attempted to open a new passage through Eichsfeld and Thuringia, into the territories of the League. He had already reached Duderstadt, when Tilly, by forced marches, came up with him. As the army of Tilly, which had been reinforced by some of Wallenstein's regiments, was superior in numbers to his own, the king, to avoid a battle, retreated towards Brunswick. But Tilly incessantly harassed his retreat, and after three days' skirmishing, he was at length obliged to await the enemy near the village of Lutter in Barenberg. The Danes began the attack with great bravery, and thrice did their intrepid monarch lead them in person against the enemy; but at length the superior numbers and discipline of the Imperialists prevailed, and the general of the League obtained a complete victory. The Danes lost sixty standards, and their whole artillery, baggage, and ammunition. Several officers of distinction and about 4,000 men were killed in the field of battle; and several companies of foot, in the flight, who had thrown themselves into the town-house of Lutter, laid down their arms and surrendered to the conqueror.

The king fled with his cavalry, and soon collected the wreck of his army which had survived this serious defeat. Tilly pursued his victory, made himself master of the Weser and Brunswick, and forced the king to retire into Bremen. Rendered more cautious by defeat, the latter now stood upon the defensive; and determined at all events to prevent the enemy from crossing the Elbe. But while he threw garrisons into every tenable place, he reduced his own diminished army to inactivity; and one after another his scattered troops were either defeated or dispersed. The forces of the League, in command of the Weser, spread themselves along the Elbe and Havel, and everywhere drove the Danes before them. Tilly himself crossing the Elbe penetrated with his victorious army into Brandenburg, while Wallenstein entered Holstein to remove the seat of war to the king's own dominions.

This general had just returned from Hungary whither he had pursued Mansfeld, without being able to obstruct his march, or prevent his junction with Bethlen Gabor. Constantly persecuted by fortune, but always superior to his fate, Mansfeld had made his way against countless difficulties, through Silesia and Hungary to Transylvania, where, after all, he was not very welcome. Relying upon the assistance of England, and a powerful diversion in Lower Saxony, Gabor had again broken the truce with the Emperor. But in place of the expected diversion in his favour, Mansfeld had drawn upon himself the whole strength of Wallenstein, and instead of bringing, required, pecuniary assistance. The want of concert in the Protestant counsels cooled Gabor's ardour; and he hastened, as usual, to avert the coming storm by a speedy peace. Firmly determined, however, to break it, with the first ray of hope, he directed Mansfeld in the mean time to apply for assistance to Venice.

Cut off from Germany, and unable to support the weak remnant of his troops in Hungary, Mansfeld sold his artillery and baggage train, and disbanded his soldiers. With a few followers, he proceeded through Bosnia and Dalmatia, towards Venice. New schemes swelled his bosom; but his career was ended. Fate, which had so restlessly sported with him throughout, now prepared for him a peaceful grave in Dalmatia. Death overtook him in the vicinity of Zara in 1626, and a short time before him died the faithful companion of his fortunes, Christian, Duke of Brunswick—two men worthy of immortality, had they but been as superior to their times as they were to their adversities.

The King of Denmark, with his whole army, was unable to cope with Tilly alone; much less, therefore, with a shattered force could he hold his ground against the two imperial generals. The Danes retired from all their posts on the Weser, the Elbe, and the Havel, and the army of Wallenstein poured like a torrent into Brandenburg, Mecklenburg, Holstein and Sleswick. That general, too proud to act in conjunction with another, had dispatched Tilly across the Elbe, to watch, as he gave out, the motions of the Dutch in that quarter; but in reality that he might terminate the war against the king, and reap for himself the fruits of Tilly's conquests. Christian had now lost all his fortresses in the German States, with the exception of Gluckstadt; his armies were defeated or dispersed; no assistance came from Germany; from England, little consolation; while his confederates in Lower Saxony were at the mercy of the conqueror. The Landgrave of Hesse Cassel had been forced by Tilly, soon after the battle of Lutter, to renounce the Danish alliance. Wallenstein's formidable appearance before Berlin reduced the Elector of Brandenburgh to submission, and compelled him to recognise, as legitimate, Maximilian's title to the Palatine Electorate. The greater part of Mecklenburgh was now overrun by imperial troops; and both dukes, as adherents of the King of Denmark, placed under the ban of the empire, and driven from their dominions. The defence of the German liberties against illegal encroachments, was punished as a crime deserving the loss of all dignities and territories; and yet this was but the prelude to the still more crying enormities which shortly followed.

The secret how Wallenstein had purposed to fulfil his extravagant designs was now manifest. He had learned the lesson from Count Mansfeld; but the scholar surpassed his master. On the principle that war must support war, Mansfeld and the Duke of Brunswick had subsisted their troops by contributions levied indiscriminately on friend and enemy; but this predatory life was attended with all the inconvenience and insecurity which accompany robbery. Like a fugitive banditti, they were obliged to steal through exasperated and vigilant enemies; to roam from one end of Germany to another; to watch their opportunity with anxiety; and to abandon the most fertile territories whenever they were defended by a superior army. If Mansfeld and Duke Christian had done such great things in the face of these difficulties, what might not be expected if the obstacles were removed; when the army raised was numerous enough to overawe in itself the most powerful states of the empire; when the name of the Emperor insured impunity to every outrage; and when, under the highest authority, and at the head of an overwhelming force, the same system of warfare was pursued, which these two adventurers had hitherto adopted at their own risk, and with only an untrained multitude?

Wallenstein had all this in view when he made his bold offer to the Emperor, which now seemed extravagant to no one. The more his army was augmented, the less cause was there to fear for its subsistence, because it could irresistibly bear down upon the refractory states; the more violent its outrages, the more probable was impunity. Towards hostile states it had the plea of right; towards the favourably disposed it could allege necessity. The inequality, too, with which it dealt out its oppressions, prevented any dangerous union among the states; while the exhaustion of their territories deprived them of the power of vengeance. Thus the whole of Germany became a kind of magazine for the imperial army, and the Emperor was enabled to deal with the other states as absolutely as with his own hereditary dominions. Universal was the clamour for redress before the imperial throne; but there was nothing to fear from the revenge of the injured princes, so long as they appealed for justice. The general discontent was directed equally against the Emperor, who had lent his name to these barbarities, and the general who exceeded his power, and openly abused the authority of his master. They applied to the Emperor for protection against the outrages of his general; but Wallenstein had no sooner felt himself absolute in the army, than he threw off his obedience to his sovereign.

The exhaustion of the enemy made a speedy peace probable; yet Wallenstein continued to augment the imperial armies until they were at least 100,000 men strong. Numberless commissions to colonelcies and inferior commands, the regal pomp of the commander-in-chief, immoderate largesses to his favourites, (for he never gave less than a thousand florins,) enormous sums lavished in corrupting the court at Vienna—all this had been effected without burdening the Emperor. These immense sums were raised by the contributions levied from the lower German provinces, where no distinction was made between friend and foe; and the territories of all princes were subjected to the same system of marching and quartering, of extortion and outrage. If credit is to be given to an extravagant contemporary statement, Wallenstein, during his seven years command, had exacted not less than sixty thousand millions of dollars from one half of Germany. The greater his extortions, the greater the rewards of his soldiers, and the greater the concourse to his standard, for the world always follows fortune. His armies flourished while all the states through which they passed withered. What cared he for the detestation of the people, and the complaints of princes? His army adored him, and the very enormity of his guilt enabled him to bid defiance to its consequences.

It would be unjust to Ferdinand, were we to lay all these irregularities to his charge. Had he foreseen that he was abandoning the German States to the mercy of his officer, he would have been sensible how dangerous to himself so absolute a general would prove. The closer the connexion became between the army, and the leader from whom flowed favour and fortune, the more the ties which united both to the Emperor were relaxed. Every thing, it is true, was done in the name of the latter; but Wallenstein only availed himself of the supreme majesty of the Emperor to crush the authority of other states. His object was to depress the princes of the empire, to destroy all gradation of rank between them and the Emperor, and to elevate the power of the latter above all competition. If the Emperor were absolute in Germany, who then would be equal to the man intrusted with the execution of his will? The height to which Wallenstein had raised the imperial authority astonished even the Emperor himself; but as the greatness of the master was entirely the work of the servant, the creation of Wallenstein would necessarily sink again into nothing upon the withdrawal of its creative hand. Not without an object, therefore, did Wallenstein labour to poison the minds of the German princes against the Emperor. The more violent their hatred of Ferdinand, the more indispensable to the Emperor would become the man who alone could render their ill-will powerless. His design unquestionably was, that his sovereign should stand in fear of no one in all Germany— besides himself, the source and engine of this despotic power.

As a step towards this end, Wallenstein now demanded the cession of Mecklenburg, to be held in pledge till the repayment of his advances for the war. Ferdinand had already created him Duke of Friedland, apparently with the view of exalting his own general over Bavaria; but an ordinary recompense would not satisfy Wallenstein's ambition. In vain was this new demand, which could be granted only at the expense of two princes of the empire, actively resisted in the Imperial Council; in vain did the Spaniards, who had long been offended by his pride, oppose his elevation. The powerful support which Wallenstein had purchased from the imperial councillors prevailed, and Ferdinand was determined, at whatever cost, to secure the devotion of so indispensable a minister. For a slight offence, one of the oldest German houses was expelled from their hereditary dominions, that a creature of the Emperor might be enriched by their spoils (1628).

Wallenstein now began to assume the title of generalissimo of the Emperor by sea and land. Wismar was taken, and a firm footing gained on the Baltic. Ships were required from Poland and the Hanse towns to carry the war to the other side of the Baltic; to pursue the Danes into the heart of their own country, and to compel them to a peace which might prepare the way to more important conquests. The communication between the Lower German States and the Northern powers would be broken, could the Emperor place himself between them, and encompass Germany, from the Adriatic to the Sound, (the intervening kingdom of Poland being already dependent on him,) with an unbroken line of territory. If such was the Emperor's plan, Wallenstein had a peculiar interest in its execution. These possessions on the Baltic should, he intended, form the first foundation of a power, which had long been the object of his ambition, and which should enable him to throw off his dependence on the Emperor.

To effect this object, it was of extreme importance to gain possession of Stralsund, a town on the Baltic. Its excellent harbour, and the short passage from it to the Swedish and Danish coasts, peculiarly fitted it for a naval station in a war with these powers. This town, the sixth of the Hanseatic League, enjoyed great privileges under the Duke of Pomerania, and totally independent of Denmark, had taken no share in the war. But neither its neutrality, nor its privileges, could protect it against the encroachments of Wallenstein, when he had once cast a longing look upon it.

The request he made, that Stralsund should receive an imperial garrison, had been firmly and honourably rejected by the magistracy, who also refused his cunningly demanded permission to march his troops through the town, Wallenstein, therefore, now proposed to besiege it.

The independence of Stralsund, as securing the free navigation of the Baltic, was equally important to the two Northern kings. A common danger overcame at last the private jealousies which had long divided these princes. In a treaty concluded at Copenhagen in 1628, they bound themselves to assist Stralsund with their combined force, and to oppose in common every foreign power which should appear in the Baltic with hostile views. Christian IV. also threw a sufficient garrison into Stralsund, and by his personal presence animated the courage of the citizens. Some ships of war which Sigismund, King of Poland, had sent to the assistance of the imperial general, were sunk by the Danish fleet; and as Lubeck refused him the use of its shipping, this imperial generalissimo of the sea had not even ships enough to blockade this single harbour.

Nothing could appear more adventurous than to attempt the conquest of a strongly fortified seaport without first blockading its harbour. Wallenstein, however, who as yet had never experienced a check, wished to conquer nature itself, and to perform impossibilities. Stralsund, open to the sea, continued to be supplied with provisions and reinforcements; yet Wallenstein maintained his blockade on the land side, and endeavoured, by boasting menaces, to supply his want of real strength. "I will take this town," said he, "though it were fastened by a chain to the heavens." The Emperor himself, who might have cause to regret an enterprise which promised no very glorious result, joyfully availed himself of the apparent submission and acceptable propositions of the inhabitants, to order the general to retire from the town. Wallenstein despised the command, and continued to harass the besieged by incessant assaults. As the Danish garrison, already much reduced, was unequal to the fatigues of this prolonged defence, and the king was unable to detach any further troops to their support, Stralsund, with Christian's consent, threw itself under the protection of the King of Sweden. The Danish commander left the town to make way for a Swedish governor, who gloriously defended it. Here Wallenstein's good fortune forsook him; and, for the first time, his pride experienced the humiliation of relinquishing his prey, after the loss of many months and of 12,000 men. The necessity to which he reduced the town of applying for protection to Sweden, laid the foundation of a close alliance between Gustavus Adolphus and Stralsund, which greatly facilitated the entrance of the Swedes into Germany.

Hitherto invariable success had attended the arms of the Emperor and the League, and Christian IV., defeated in Germany, had sought refuge in his own islands; but the Baltic checked the further progress of the conquerors. The want of ships not only stopped the pursuit of the king, but endangered their previous acquisitions. The union of the two northern monarchs was most to be dreaded, because, so long as it lasted, it effectually prevented the Emperor and his general from acquiring a footing on the Baltic, or effecting a landing in Sweden. But if they could succeed in dissolving this union, and especially securing the friendship of the Danish king, they might hope to overpower the insulated force of Sweden. The dread of the interference of foreign powers, the insubordination of the Protestants in his own states, and still more the storm which was gradually darkening along the whole of Protestant Germany, inclined the Emperor to peace, which his general, from opposite motives, was equally desirous to effect. Far from wishing for a state of things which would reduce him from the meridian of greatness and glory to the obscurity of private life, he only wished to change the theatre of war, and by a partial peace to prolong the general confusion. The friendship of Denmark, whose neighbour he had become as Duke of Mecklenburgh, was most important for the success of his ambitious views; and he resolved, even at the sacrifice of his sovereign's interests, to secure its alliance.

By the treaty of Copenhagen, Christian IV. had expressly engaged not to conclude a separate peace with the Emperor, without the consent of Sweden. Notwithstanding, Wallenstein's proposition was readily received by him. In a conference at Lubeck in 1629, from which Wallenstein, with studied contempt, excluded the Swedish ambassadors who came to intercede for Mecklenburgh, all the conquests taken by the imperialists were restored to the Danes. The conditions imposed upon the king were, that he should interfere no farther with the affairs of Germany than was called for by his character of Duke of Holstein; that he should on no pretext harass the Chapters of Lower Germany, and should leave the Dukes of Mecklenburgh to their fate. By Christian himself had these princes been involved in the war with the Emperor; he now sacrificed them, to gain the favour of the usurper of their territories. Among the motives which had engaged him in a war with the Emperor, not the least was the restoration of his relation, the Elector Palatine—yet the name of that unfortunate prince was not even mentioned in the treaty; while in one of its articles the legitimacy of the Bavarian election was expressly recognised. Thus meanly and ingloriously did Christian IV. retire from the field.

Ferdinand had it now in his power, for the second time, to secure the tranquillity of Germany; and it depended solely on his will whether the treaty with Denmark should or should not be the basis of a general peace. From every quarter arose the cry of the unfortunate, petitioning for an end of their sufferings; the cruelties of his soldiers, and the rapacity of his generals, had exceeded all bounds. Germany, laid waste by the desolating bands of Mansfeld and the Duke of Brunswick, and by the still more terrible hordes of Tilly and Wallenstein, lay exhausted, bleeding, wasted, and sighing for repose. An anxious desire for peace was felt by all conditions, and by the Emperor himself; involved as he was in a war with France in Upper Italy, exhausted by his past warfare in Germany, and apprehensive of the day of reckoning which was approaching. But, unfortunately, the conditions on which alone the two religious parties were willing respectively to sheath the sword, were irreconcileable. The Roman Catholics wished to terminate the war to their own advantage; the Protestants advanced equal pretensions. The Emperor, instead of uniting both parties by a prudent moderation, sided with one; and thus Germany was again plunged in the horrors of a bloody war.

From the very close of the Bohemian troubles, Ferdinand had carried on a counter reformation in his hereditary dominions, in which, however, from regard to some of the Protestant Estates, he proceeded, at first, with moderation. But the victories of his generals in Lower Germany encouraged him to throw off all reserve. Accordingly he had it intimated to all the Protestants in these dominions, that they must either abandon their religion, or their native country,—a bitter and dreadful alternative, which excited the most violent commotions among his Austrian subjects. In the Palatinate, immediately after the expulsion of Frederick, the Protestant religion had been suppressed, and its professors expelled from the University of Heidelberg.

All this was but the prelude to greater changes. In the Electoral Congress held at Muehlhausen, the Roman Catholics had demanded of the Emperor that all the archbishoprics, bishoprics, mediate and immediate, abbacies and monasteries, which, since the Diet of Augsburg, had been secularized by the Protestants, should be restored to the church, in order to indemnify them for the losses and sufferings in the war. To a Roman Catholic prince so zealous as Ferdinand was, such a hint was not likely to be neglected; but he still thought it would be premature to arouse the whole Protestants of Germany by so decisive a step. Not a single Protestant prince but would be deprived, by this revocation of the religious foundations, of a part of his lands; for where these revenues had not actually been diverted to secular purposes they had been made over to the Protestant church. To this source, many princes owed the chief part of their revenues and importance. All, without exception, would be irritated by this demand for restoration. The religious treaty did not expressly deny their right to these chapters, although it did not allow it. But a possession which had now been held for nearly a century, the silence of four preceding emperors, and the law of equity, which gave them an equal right with the Roman Catholics to the foundations of their common ancestors, might be strongly pleaded by them as a valid title. Besides the actual loss of power and authority, which the surrender of these foundations would occasion, besides the inevitable confusion which would necessarily attend it, one important disadvantage to which it would lead, was, that the restoration of the Roman Catholic bishops would increase the strength of that party in the Diet by so many additional votes. Such grievous sacrifices likely to fall on the Protestants, made the Emperor apprehensive of a formidable opposition; and until the military ardour should have cooled in Germany, he had no wish to provoke a party formidable by its union, and which in the Elector of Saxony had a powerful leader. He resolved, therefore, to try the experiment at first on a small scale, in order to ascertain how it was likely to succeed on a larger one. Accordingly, some of the free cities in Upper Germany, and the Duke of Wirtemberg, received orders to surrender to the Roman Catholics several of the confiscated chapters.

The state of affairs in Saxony enabled the Emperor to make some bolder experiments in that quarter. In the bishoprics of Magdeburg and Halberstadt, the Protestant canons had not hesitated to elect bishops of their own religion. Both bishoprics, with the exception of the town of Magdeburg itself, were overrun by the troops of Wallenstein. It happened, moreover, that by the death of the Administrator Duke Christian of Brunswick, Halberstadt was vacant, as was also the Archbishopric of Magdeburg by the deposition of Christian William, a prince of the House of Brandenburgh. Ferdinand took advantage of the circumstance to restore the see of Halberstadt to a Roman Catholic bishop, and a prince of his own house. To avoid a similar coercion, the Chapter of Magdeburg hastened to elect a son of the Elector of Saxony as archbishop. But the pope, who with his arrogated authority interfered in this matter, conferred the Archbishopric of Magdeburg also on the Austrian prince. Thus, with all his pious zeal for religion, Ferdinand never lost sight of the interests of his family.

At length, when the peace of Lubeck had delivered the Emperor from all apprehensions on the side of Denmark, and the German Protestants seemed entirely powerless, the League becoming louder and more urgent in its demands, Ferdinand, in 1629, signed the Edict of Restitution, (so famous by its disastrous consequences,) which he had previously laid before the four Roman Catholic electors for their approbation. In the preamble, he claimed the prerogative, in right of his imperial authority, to interpret the meaning of the religious treaty, the ambiguities of which had already caused so many disputes, and to decide as supreme arbiter and judge between the contending parties. This prerogative he founded upon the practice of his ancestors, and its previous recognition even by Protestant states. Saxony had actually acknowledged this right of the Emperor; and it now became evident how deeply this court had injured the Protestant cause by its dependence on the House of Austria. But though the meaning of the religious treaty was really ambiguous, as a century of religious disputes sufficiently proved, yet for the Emperor, who must be either a Protestant or a Roman Catholic, and therefore an interested party, to assume the right of deciding between the disputants, was clearly a violation of an essential article of the pacification. He could not be judge in his own cause, without reducing the liberties of the empire to an empty sound.

And now, in virtue of this usurpation, Ferdinand decided, "That every secularization of a religious foundation, mediate or immediate, by the Protestants, subsequent to the date of the treaty, was contrary to its spirit, and must be revoked as a breach of it." He further decided, "That, by the religious peace, Catholic proprietors of estates were no further bound to their Protestant subjects than to allow them full liberty to quit their territories." In obedience to this decision, all unlawful possessors of benefices—the Protestant states in short without exception—were ordered, under pain of the ban of the empire, immediately to surrender their usurped possessions to the imperial commissioners.

This sentence applied to no less than two archbishoprics and twelve bishoprics, besides innumerable abbacies. The edict came like a thunderbolt on the whole of Protestant Germany; dreadful even in its immediate consequences; but yet more so from the further calamities it seemed to threaten. The Protestants were now convinced that the suppression of their religion had been resolved on by the Emperor and the League, and that the overthrow of German liberty would soon follow. Their remonstrances were unheeded; the commissioners were named, and an army assembled to enforce obedience. The edict was first put in force in Augsburg, where the treaty was concluded; the city was again placed under the government of its bishop, and six Protestant churches in the town were closed. The Duke of Wirtemberg was, in like manner, compelled to surrender his abbacies. These severe measures, though they alarmed the Protestant states, were yet insufficient to rouse them to an active resistance. Their fear of the Emperor was too strong, and many were disposed to quiet submission. The hope of attaining their end by gentle measures, induced the Roman Catholics likewise to delay for a year the execution of the edict, and this saved the Protestants; before the end of that period, the success of the Swedish arms had totally changed the state of affairs.

In a Diet held at Ratisbon, at which Ferdinand was present in person (in 1630), the necessity of taking some measures for the immediate restoration of a general peace to Germany, and for the removal of all grievances, was debated. The complaints of the Roman Catholics were scarcely less numerous than those of the Protestants, although Ferdinand had flattered himself that by the Edict of Restitution he had secured the members of the League, and its leader by the gift of the electoral dignity, and the cession of great part of the Palatinate. But the good understanding between the Emperor and the princes of the League had rapidly declined since the employment of Wallenstein. Accustomed to give law to Germany, and even to sway the Emperor's own destiny, the haughty Elector of Bavaria now at once saw himself supplanted by the imperial general, and with that of the League, his own importance completely undermined. Another had now stepped in to reap the fruits of his victories, and to bury his past services in oblivion. Wallenstein's imperious character, whose dearest triumph was in degrading the authority of the princes, and giving an odious latitude to that of the Emperor, tended not a little to augment the irritation of the Elector. Discontented with the Emperor, and distrustful of his intentions, he had entered into an alliance with France, which the other members of the League were suspected of favouring. A fear of the Emperor's plans of aggrandizement, and discontent with existing evils, had extinguished among them all feelings of gratitude. Wallenstein's exactions had become altogether intolerable. Brandenburg estimated its losses at twenty, Pomerania at ten, Hesse Cassel at seven millions of dollars, and the rest in proportion. The cry for redress was loud, urgent, and universal; all prejudices were hushed; Roman Catholics and Protestants were united on this point. The terrified Emperor was assailed on all sides by petitions against Wallenstein, and his ear filled with the most fearful descriptions of his outrages. Ferdinand was not naturally cruel. If not totally innocent of the atrocities which were practised in Germany under the shelter of his name, he was ignorant of their extent; and he was not long in yielding to the representation of the princes, and reduced his standing army by eighteen thousand cavalry. While this reduction took place, the Swedes were actively preparing an expedition into Germany, and the greater part of the disbanded Imperialists enlisted under their banners.

The Emperor's concessions only encouraged the Elector of Bavaria to bolder demands. So long as the Duke of Friedland retained the supreme command, his triumph over the Emperor was incomplete. The princes of the League were meditating a severe revenge on Wallenstein for that haughtiness with which he had treated them all alike. His dismissal was demanded by the whole college of electors, and even by Spain, with a degree of unanimity and urgency which astonished the Emperor. The anxiety with which Wallenstein's enemies pressed for his dismissal, ought to have convinced the Emperor of the importance of his services. Wallenstein, informed of the cabals which were forming against him in Ratisbon, lost no time in opening the eyes of the Emperor to the real views of the Elector of Bavaria. He himself appeared in Ratisbon, with a pomp which threw his master into the shade, and increased the hatred of his opponents.

Long was the Emperor undecided. The sacrifice demanded was a painful one. To the Duke of Friedland alone he owed his preponderance; he felt how much he would lose in yielding him to the indignation of the princes. But at this moment, unfortunately, he was under the necessity of conciliating the Electors. His son Ferdinand had already been chosen King of Hungary, and he was endeavouring to procure his election as his successor in the empire. For this purpose, the support of Maximilian was indispensable. This consideration was the weightiest, and to oblige the Elector of Bavaria he scrupled not to sacrifice his most valuable servant.

At the Diet at Ratisbon, there were present ambassadors from France, empowered to adjust the differences which seemed to menace a war in Italy between the Emperor and their sovereign. Vincent, Duke of Mantua and Montferrat, dying without issue, his next relation, Charles, Duke of Nevers, had taken possession of this inheritance, without doing homage to the Emperor as liege lord of the principality. Encouraged by the support of France and Venice, he refused to surrender these territories into the hands of the imperial commissioners, until his title to them should be decided. On the other hand, Ferdinand had taken up arms at the instigation of the Spaniards, to whom, as possessors of Milan, the near neighbourhood of a vassal of France was peculiarly alarming, and who welcomed this prospect of making, with the assistance of the Emperor, additional conquests in Italy. In spite of all the exertions of Pope Urban VIII. to avert a war in that country, Ferdinand marched a German army across the Alps, and threw the Italian states into a general consternation. His arms had been successful throughout Germany, and exaggerated fears revived the olden apprehension of Austria's projects of universal monarchy. All the horrors of the German war now spread like a deluge over those favoured countries which the Po waters; Mantua was taken by storm, and the surrounding districts given up to the ravages of a lawless soldiery. The curse of Italy was thus added to the maledictions upon the Emperor which resounded through Germany; and even in the Roman Conclave, silent prayers were offered for the success of the Protestant arms.

Alarmed by the universal hatred which this Italian campaign had drawn upon him, and wearied out by the urgent remonstrances of the Electors, who zealously supported the application of the French ambassador, the Emperor promised the investiture to the new Duke of Mantua.

This important service on the part of Bavaria, of course, required an equivalent from France. The adjustment of the treaty gave the envoys of Richelieu, during their residence in Ratisbon, the desired opportunity of entangling the Emperor in dangerous intrigues, of inflaming the discontented princes of the League still more strongly against him, and of turning to his disadvantage all the transactions of the Diet. For this purpose Richelieu had chosen an admirable instrument in Father Joseph, a Capuchin friar, who accompanied the ambassadors without exciting the least suspicion. One of his principal instructions was assiduously to bring about the dismissal of Wallenstein. With the general who had led it to victory, the army of Austria would lose its principal strength; many armies could not compensate for the loss of this individual. It would therefore be a masterstroke of policy, at the very moment when a victorious monarch, the absolute master of his operations, was arming against the Emperor, to remove from the head of the imperial armies the only general who, by ability and military experience, was able to cope with the French king. Father Joseph, in the interests of Bavaria, undertook to overcome the irresolution of the Emperor, who was now in a manner besieged by the Spaniards and the Electoral Council. "It would be expedient," he thought, "to gratify the Electors on this occasion, and thereby facilitate his son's election to the Roman Crown. This object once gained, Wallenstein could at any time resume his former station." The artful Capuchin was too sure of his man to touch upon this ground of consolation.

The voice of a monk was to Ferdinand II. the voice of God. "Nothing on earth," writes his own confessor, "was more sacred in his eyes than a priest. If it could happen, he used to say, that an angel and a Regular were to meet him at the same time and place, the Regular should receive his first, and the angel his second obeisance." Wallenstein's dismissal was determined upon.

In return for this pious concession, the Capuchin dexterously counteracted the Emperor's scheme to procure for the King of Hungary the further dignity of King of the Romans. In an express clause of the treaty just concluded, the French ministers engaged in the name of their sovereign to observe a complete neutrality between the Emperor and his enemies; while, at the same time, Richelieu was actually negociating with the King of Sweden to declare war, and pressing upon him the alliance of his master. The latter, indeed, disavowed the lie as soon as it had served its purpose, and Father Joseph, confined to a convent, must atone for the alleged offence of exceeding his instructions. Ferdinand perceived, when too late, that he had been imposed upon. "A wicked Capuchin," he was heard to say, "has disarmed me with his rosary, and thrust nothing less than six electoral crowns into his cowl."

Artifice and trickery thus triumphed over the Emperor, at the moment when he was believed to be omnipotent in Germany, and actually was so in the field. With the loss of 18,000 men, and of a general who alone was worth whole armies, he left Ratisbon without gaining the end for which he had made such sacrifices. Before the Swedes had vanquished him in the field, Maximilian of Bavaria and Father Joseph had given him a mortal blow. At this memorable Diet at Ratisbon the war with Sweden was resolved upon, and that of Mantua terminated. Vainly had the princes present at it interceded for the Dukes of Mecklenburgh; and equally fruitless had been an application by the English ambassadors for a pension to the Palatine Frederick.

Wallenstein was at the head of an army of nearly a hundred thousand men who adored him, when the sentence of his dismissal arrived. Most of the officers were his creatures:—with the common soldiers his hint was law. His ambition was boundless, his pride indomitable, his imperious spirit could not brook an injury unavenged. One moment would now precipitate him from the height of grandeur into the obscurity of a private station. To execute such a sentence upon such a delinquent seemed to require more address than it cost to obtain it from the judge. Accordingly, two of Wallenstein's most intimate friends were selected as heralds of these evil tidings, and instructed to soften them as much as possible, by flattering assurances of the continuance of the Emperor's favour.

Wallenstein had ascertained the purport of their message before the imperial ambassadors arrived. He had time to collect himself, and his countenance exhibited an external calmness, while grief and rage were storming in his bosom. He had made up his mind to obey. The Emperor's decision had taken him by surprise before circumstances were ripe, or his preparations complete, for the bold measures he had contemplated. His extensive estates were scattered over Bohemia and Moravia; and by their confiscation, the Emperor might at once destroy the sinews of his power. He looked, therefore, to the future for revenge; and in this hope he was encouraged by the predictions of an Italian astrologer, who led his imperious spirit like a child in leading strings. Seni had read in the stars, that his master's brilliant career was not yet ended; and that bright and glorious prospects still awaited him. It was, indeed, unnecessary to consult the stars to foretell that an enemy, Gustavus Adolphus, would ere long render indispensable the services of such a general as Wallenstein.

"The Emperor is betrayed," said Wallenstein to the messengers; "I pity but forgive him. It is plain that the grasping spirit of the Bavarian dictates to him. I grieve that, with so much weakness, he has sacrificed me, but I will obey." He dismissed the emissaries with princely presents; and in a humble letter besought the continuance of the Emperor's favour, and of the dignities he had bestowed upon him.

The murmurs of the army were universal, on hearing of the dismissal of their general; and the greater part of his officers immediately quitted the imperial service. Many followed him to his estates in Bohemia and Moravia; others he attached to his interests by pensions, in order to command their services when the opportunity should offer.

But repose was the last thing that Wallenstein contemplated when he returned to private life. In his retreat, he surrounded himself with a regal pomp, which seemed to mock the sentence of degradation. Six gates led to the palace he inhabited in Prague, and a hundred houses were pulled down to make way for his courtyard. Similar palaces were built on his other numerous estates. Gentlemen of the noblest houses contended for the honour of serving him, and even imperial chamberlains resigned the golden key to the Emperor, to fill a similar office under Wallenstein. He maintained sixty pages, who were instructed by the ablest masters. His antichamber was protected by fifty life guards. His table never consisted of less than 100 covers, and his seneschal was a person of distinction. When he travelled, his baggage and suite accompanied him in a hundred wagons, drawn by six or four horses; his court followed in sixty carriages, attended by fifty led horses. The pomp of his liveries, the splendour of his equipages, and the decorations of his apartments, were in keeping with all the rest. Six barons and as many knights, were in constant attendance about his person, and ready to execute his slightest order. Twelve patrols went their rounds about his palace, to prevent any disturbance. His busy genius required silence. The noise of coaches was to be kept away from his residence, and the streets leading to it were frequently blocked up with chains. His own circle was as silent as the approaches to his palace; dark, reserved, and impenetrable, he was more sparing of his words than of his gifts; while the little that he spoke was harsh and imperious. He never smiled, and the coldness of his temperament was proof against sensual seductions. Ever occupied with grand schemes, he despised all those idle amusements in which so many waste their lives. The correspondence he kept up with the whole of Europe was chiefly managed by himself, and, that as little as possible might be trusted to the silence of others, most of the letters were written by his own hand. He was a man of large stature, thin, of a sallow complexion, with short red hair, and small sparkling eyes. A gloomy and forbidding seriousness sat upon his brow; and his magnificent presents alone retained the trembling crowd of his dependents.

In this stately obscurity did Wallenstein silently, but not inactively, await the hour of revenge. The victorious career of Gustavus Adolphus soon gave him a presentiment of its approach. Not one of his lofty schemes had been abandoned; and the Emperor's ingratitude had loosened the curb of his ambition. The dazzling splendour of his private life bespoke high soaring projects; and, lavish as a king, he seemed already to reckon among his certain possessions those which he contemplated with hope.

After Wallenstein's dismissal, and the invasion of Gustavus Adolphus, a new generalissimo was to be appointed; and it now appeared advisable to unite both the imperial army and that of the League under one general. Maximilian of Bavaria sought this appointment, which would have enabled him to dictate to the Emperor, who, from a conviction of this, wished to procure the command for his eldest son, the King of Hungary. At last, in order to avoid offence to either of the competitors, the appointment was given to Tilly, who now exchanged the Bavarian for the Austrian service. The imperial army in Germany, after the retirement of Wallenstein, amounted to about 40,000 men; that of the League to nearly the same number, both commanded by excellent officers, trained by the experience of several campaigns, and proud of a long series of victories. With such a force, little apprehension was felt at the invasion of the King of Sweden, and the less so as it commanded both

Pomerania and Mecklenburg, the only countries through which he could enter Germany.

After the unsuccessful attempt of the King of Denmark to check the Emperor's progress, Gustavus Adolphus was the only prince in Europe from whom oppressed liberty could look for protection—the only one who, while he was personally qualified to conduct such an enterprise, had both political motives to recommend and wrongs to justify it. Before the commencement of the war in Lower Saxony, important political interests induced him, as well as the King of Denmark, to offer his services and his army for the defence of Germany; but the offer of the latter had, to his own misfortune, been preferred. Since that time, Wallenstein and the Emperor had adopted measures which must have been equally offensive to him as a man and as a king. Imperial troops had been despatched to the aid of the Polish king, Sigismund, to defend Prussia against the Swedes. When the king complained to Wallenstein of this act of hostility, he received for answer, "The Emperor has more soldiers than he wants for himself, he must help his friends." The Swedish ambassadors had been insolently ordered by Wallenstein to withdraw from the conference at Lubeck; and when, unawed by this command, they were courageous enough to remain, contrary to the law of nations, he had threatened them with violence. Ferdinand had also insulted the Swedish flag, and intercepted the king's despatches to Transylvania. He also threw every obstacle in the way of a peace betwixt Poland and Sweden, supported the pretensions of Sigismund to the Swedish throne, and denied the right of Gustavus to the title of king. Deigning no regard to the repeated remonstrances of Gustavus, he rather aggravated the offence by new grievances, than acceded the required satisfaction.

So many personal motives, supported by important considerations, both of policy and religion, and seconded by pressing invitations from Germany, had their full weight with a prince, who was naturally the more jealous of his royal prerogative the more it was questioned, who was flattered by the glory he hoped to gain as Protector of the Oppressed, and passionately loved war as the element of his genius. But, until a truce or peace with Poland should set his hands free, a new and dangerous war was not to be thought of.

Cardinal Richelieu had the merit of effecting this truce with Poland. This great statesman, who guided the helm of Europe, while in France he repressed the rage of faction and the insolence of the nobles, pursued steadily, amidst the cares of a stormy administration, his plan of lowering the ascendancy of the House of Austria. But circumstances opposed considerable obstacles to the execution of his designs; and even the greatest minds cannot, with impunity, defy the prejudices of the age. The minister of a Roman Catholic king, and a Cardinal, he was prevented by the purple he bore from joining the enemies of that church in an open attack on a power which had the address to sanctify its ambitious encroachments under the name of religion. The external deference which Richelieu was obliged to pay to the narrow views of his contemporaries limited his exertions to secret negociations, by which he endeavoured to gain the hand of others to accomplish the enlightened projects of his own mind. After a fruitless attempt to prevent the peace between Denmark and the Emperor, he had recourse to Gustavus Adolphus, the hero of his age. No exertion was spared to bring this monarch to a favourable decision, and at the same time to facilitate the execution of it. Charnasse, an unsuspected agent of the Cardinal, proceeded to Polish Prussia, where Gustavus Adolphus was conducting the war against Sigismund, and alternately visited these princes, in order to persuade them to a truce or peace. Gustavus had been long inclined to it, and the French minister succeeded at last in opening the eyes of Sigismund to his true interests, and to the deceitful policy of the Emperor. A truce for six years was agreed on, Gustavus being allowed to retain all his conquests. This treaty gave him also what he had so long desired, the liberty of directing his arms against the Emperor. For this the French ambassador offered him the alliance of his sovereign and considerable subsidies. But Gustavus Adolphus was justly apprehensive lest the acceptance of the assistance should make him dependent upon France, and fetter him in his career of conquest, while an alliance with a Roman Catholic power might excite distrust among the Protestants.

If the war was just and necessary, the circumstances under which it was undertaken were not less promising. The name of the Emperor, it is true, was formidable, his resources inexhaustible, his power hitherto invincible. So dangerous a contest would have dismayed any other than Gustavus. He saw all the obstacles and dangers which opposed his undertaking, but he knew also the means by which, as he hoped, they might be conquered. His army, though not numerous, was well disciplined, inured to hardship by a severe climate and campaigns, and trained to victory in the war with Poland. Sweden, though poor in men and money, and overtaxed by an eight years' war, was devoted to its monarch with an enthusiasm which assured him of the ready support of his subjects. In Germany, the name of the Emperor was at least as much hated as feared. The Protestant princes only awaited the arrival of a deliverer to throw off his intolerable yoke, and openly declare for the Swedes. Even the Roman Catholic states would welcome an antagonist to the Emperor, whose opposition might control his overwhelming influence. The first victory gained on German ground would be decisive. It would encourage those princes who still hesitated to declare themselves, strengthen the cause of his adherents, augment his troops, and open resources for the maintenance of the campaign. If the greater part of the German states were impoverished by oppression, the flourishing Hanse towns had escaped, and they could not hesitate, by a small voluntary sacrifice, to avert the general ruin. As the imperialists should be driven from the different provinces, their armies would diminish, since they were subsisting on the countries in which they were encamped. The strength, too, of the Emperor had been lessened by ill-timed detachments to Italy and the Netherlands; while Spain, weakened by the loss of the Manilla galleons, and engaged in a serious war in the Netherlands, could afford him little support. Great Britain, on the other hand, gave the King of Sweden hope of considerable subsidies; and France, now at peace with itself, came forward with the most favourable offers.

But the strongest pledge for the success of his undertaking Gustavus found—in himself. Prudence demanded that he should embrace all the foreign assistance he could, in order to guard his enterprise from the imputation of rashness; but all his confidence and courage were entirely derived from himself. He was indisputably the greatest general of his age, and the bravest soldier in the army which he had formed. Familiar with the tactics of Greece and Rome, he had discovered a more effective system of warfare, which was adopted as a model by the most eminent commanders of subsequent times. He reduced the unwieldy squadrons of cavalry, and rendered their movements more light and rapid; and, with the same view, he widened the intervals between his battalions. Instead of the usual array in a single line, he disposed his forces in two lines, that the second might advance in the event of the first giving way.

He made up for his want of cavalry, by placing infantry among the horse; a practice which frequently decided the victory. Europe first learned from him the importance of infantry. All Germany was astonished at the strict discipline which, at the first, so creditably distinguished the Swedish army within their territories; all disorders were punished with the utmost severity, particularly impiety, theft, gambling, and duelling. The Swedish articles of war enforced frugality. In the camp, the King's tent not excepted, neither silver nor gold was to be seen. The general's eye looked as vigilantly to the morals as to the martial bravery of his soldiers; every regiment was ordered to form round its chaplain for morning and evening prayers. In all these points the lawgiver was also an example. A sincere and ardent piety exalted his courage. Equally free from the coarse infidelity which leaves the passions of the barbarian without a control,—and from the grovelling superstition of Ferdinand, who humbled himself to the dust before the Supreme Being, while he haughtily trampled on his fellow-creature—in the height of his success he was ever a man and a Christian—in the height of his devotion, a king and a hero. The hardships of war he shared with the meanest soldier in his army; maintained a calm serenity amidst the hottest fury of battle; his glance was omnipresent, and he intrepidly forgot the danger while he exposed himself to the greatest peril. His natural courage, indeed, too often made him forget the duty of a general; and the life of a king ended in the death of a common soldier. But such a leader was followed to victory alike by the coward and the brave, and his eagle glance marked every heroic deed which his example had inspired. The fame of their sovereign excited in the nation an enthusiastic sense of their own importance; proud of their king, the peasant in Finland and Gothland joyfully contributed his pittance; the soldier willingly shed his blood; and the lofty energy which his single mind had imparted to the nation long survived its creator.

The necessity of the war was acknowledged, but the best plan of conducting it was a matter of much question. Even to the bold Chancellor Oxenstiern, an offensive war appeared too daring a measure; the resources of his poor and conscientious master, appeared to him too slender to compete with those of a despotic sovereign, who held all Germany at his command. But the minister's timid scruples were overruled by the hero's penetrating prudence. "If we await the enemy in Sweden," said Gustavus, "in the event of a defeat every thing would be lost, by a fortunate commencement in Germany everything would be gained. The sea is wide, and we have a long line of coast in Sweden to defend. If the enemy's fleet should escape us, or our own be defeated, it would, in either case, be impossible to prevent the enemy's landing. Every thing depends on the retention of Stralsund. So long as this harbour is open to us, we shall both command the Baltic, and secure a retreat from Germany. But to protect this port, we must not remain in Sweden, but advance at once into Pomerania. Let us talk no more, then, of a defensive war, by which we should sacrifice our greatest advantages. Sweden must not be doomed to behold a hostile banner; if we are vanquished in Germany, it will be time enough to follow your plan."

Gustavus resolved to cross the Baltic and attack the Emperor. His preparations were made with the utmost expedition, and his precautionary measures were not less prudent than the resolution itself was bold and magnanimous. Before engaging in so distant a war, it was necessary to secure Sweden against its neighbours. At a personal interview with the King of Denmark at Markaroed, Gustavus assured himself of the friendship of that monarch; his frontier on the side of Moscow was well guarded; Poland might be held in check from Germany, if it betrayed any design of infringing the truce. Falkenberg, a Swedish ambassador, who visited the courts of Holland and Germany, obtained the most flattering promises from several Protestant princes, though none of them yet possessed courage or self-devotion enough to enter into a formal alliance with him. Lubeck and Hamburg engaged to advance him money, and to accept Swedish copper in return. Emissaries were also despatched to the Prince of Transylvania, to excite that implacable enemy of Austria to arms.

In the mean time, Swedish levies were made in Germany and the Netherlands, the regiments increased to their full complement, new ones raised, transports provided, a fleet fitted out, provisions, military stores, and money collected. Thirty ships of war were in a short time prepared, 15,000 men equipped, and 200 transports were ready to convey them across the Baltic. A greater force Gustavus Adolphus was unwilling to carry into Germany, and even the maintenance of this exceeded the revenues of his kingdom. But however small his army, it was admirable in all points of discipline, courage, and experience, and might serve as the nucleus of a more powerful armament, if it once gained the German frontier, and its first attempts were attended with success. Oxenstiern, at once general and chancellor, was posted with 10,000 men in Prussia, to protect that province against Poland. Some regular troops, and a considerable body of militia, which served as a nursery for the main body, remained in Sweden, as a defence against a sudden invasion by any treacherous neighbour.

These were the measures taken for the external defence of the kingdom. Its internal administration was provided for with equal care. The government was intrusted to the Council of State, and the finances to the Palatine John Casimir, the brother-in-law of the King, while his wife, tenderly as he was attached to her, was excluded from all share in the government, for which her limited talents incapacitated her. He set his house in order like a dying man. On the 20th May, 1630, when all his measures were arranged, and all was ready for his departure, the King appeared in the Diet at Stockholm, to bid the States a solemn farewell. Taking in his arms his daughter Christina, then only four years old, who, in the cradle, had been acknowledged as his successor, he presented her to the States as the future sovereign, exacted from them a renewal of the oath of allegiance to her, in case he should never more return; and then read the ordinances for the government of the kingdom during his absence, or the minority of his daughter. The whole assembly was dissolved in tears, and the King himself was some time before he could attain sufficient composure to deliver his farewell address to the States.

"Not lightly or wantonly," said he, "am I about to involve myself and you in this new and dangerous war; God is my witness that *I* do not fight to gratify my own ambition. But the Emperor has wronged me most shamefully in the person of my ambassadors. He has supported my enemies, persecuted my friends and brethren, trampled my religion in the dust, and even stretched his revengeful arm against my crown. The oppressed states of Germany call loudly for aid, which, by God's help, we will give them.

"I am fully sensible of the dangers to which my life will be exposed. I have never yet shrunk from them, nor is it likely that I shall escape them all. Hitherto, Providence has wonderfully protected me, but I shall at last fall in defence of my country. I commend you to the protection of Heaven. Be just, be conscientious, act uprightly, and we shall meet again in eternity.

"To you, my Counsellors of State, I address myself first. May God enlighten you, and fill you with wisdom, to promote the welfare of my people. You, too, my brave nobles, I commend to the divine protection. Continue to prove yourselves the worthy successors of those Gothic heroes, whose bravery humbled to the dust the pride of ancient Rome. To you, ministers of religion, I recommend moderation and unity; be yourselves examples of the virtues which you preach, and abuse not your influence over the minds of my people. On you, deputies of the burgesses, and the peasantry, I entreat the blessing of heaven; may your industry be rewarded by a prosperous harvest; your stores plenteously filled, and may you be crowned abundantly with all the blessings of this life. For the prosperity of all my subjects, absent and present, I offer my warmest prayers to Heaven. I bid you all a sincere—it may be — an eternal farewell."

The embarkation of the troops took place at Elfsknaben, where the fleet lay at anchor. An immense concourse flocked thither to witness this magnificent spectacle. The hearts of the spectators were agitated by varied emotions, as they alternately considered the vastness of the enterprise, and the greatness of the leader. Among the superior officers who commanded in this army were Gustavus Horn, the Rhinegrave Otto Lewis, Henry Matthias, Count Thurn, Ottenberg, Baudissen, Banner, Teufel, Tott, Mutsenfahl, Falkenberg, Kniphausen, and other distinguished names. Detained by contrary winds, the fleet did not sail till June, and on the 24th of that month reached the Island of Rugen in Pomerania.

Gustavus Adolphus was the first who landed. In the presence of his suite, he knelt on the shore of Germany to return thanks to the Almighty for the safe arrival of his fleet and his army. He landed his troops on the Islands of Wollin and Usedom; upon his approach, the imperial garrisons abandoned their entrenchments and fled. He advanced rapidly on Stettin, to secure this important place before the appearance of the Imperialists. Bogislaus XIV., Duke of Pomerania, a feeble and superannuated prince, had been long tired out by the outrages committed by the latter within his territories; but too weak to resist, he had contented himself with murmurs. The appearance of his deliverer, instead of animating his courage, increased his fear and anxiety. Severely as his country had suffered from the Imperialists, the risk of incurring the Emperor's vengeance prevented him from declaring openly for the Swedes. Gustavus Adolphus, who was encamped under the walls of the town, summoned the city to receive a Swedish garrison. Bogislaus appeared in person in the camp of Gustavus, to deprecate this condition. "I come to you," said Gustavus, "not as an enemy but a friend. I wage no war against Pomerania, nor against the German empire, but against the enemies of both.

In my hands this duchy shall be sacred; and it shall be restored to you at the conclusion of the campaign, by me, with more certainty, than by any other. Look to the traces of the imperial force within your territories, and to mine in Usedom; and decide whether you will have the Emperor or me as your friend. What have you to expect, if the Emperor should make himself master of your capital? Will he deal with you more leniently than I? Or is it your intention to stop my progress? The case is pressing: decide at once, and do not compel me to have recourse to more violent measures."

The alternative was a painful one. On the one side, the King of Sweden was before his gates with a formidable army; on the other, he saw the inevitable vengeance of the Emperor, and the fearful example of so many German princes, who were now wandering in misery, the victims of that revenge. The more immediate danger decided his resolution. The gates of Stettin were opened to the king; the Swedish troops entered; and the Austrians, who were advancing by rapid marches, anticipated. The capture of this place procured for the king a firm footing in Pomerania, the command of the Oder, and a magazine for his troops. To prevent a charge of treachery, Bogislaus was careful to excuse this step to the Emperor on the plea of necessity; but aware of Ferdinand's implacable disposition, he entered into a close alliance with his new protector. By this league with Pomerania, Gustavus secured a powerful friend in Germany, who covered his rear, and maintained his communication with Sweden.

As Ferdinand was already the aggressor in Prussia, Gustavus Adolphus thought himself absolved from the usual formalities, and commenced hostilities without any declaration of war. To the other European powers, he justified his conduct in a manifesto, in which he detailed the grounds which had led him to take up arms. Meanwhile he continued his progress in Pomerania, while he saw his army daily increasing. The troops which had fought under Mansfeld, Duke Christian of Brunswick, the King of Denmark, and Wallenstein, came in crowds, both officers and soldiers, to join his victorious standard.

At the Imperial court, the invasion of the king of Sweden at first excited far less attention than it merited. The pride of Austria, extravagantly elated by its unheard-of successes, looked down with contempt upon a prince, who, with a handful of men, came from an obscure corner of Europe, and who owed his past successes, as they imagined, entirely to the incapacity of a weak opponent. The depreciatory representation which Wallenstein had artfully given of the Swedish power, increased the Emperor's security; for what had he to fear from an enemy, whom his general undertook to drive with such ease from Germany? Even the rapid progress of Gustavus Adolphus in Pomerania, could not entirely dispel this prejudice, which the mockeries of the courtiers continued to feed. He was called in Vienna the Snow King, whom the cold of the north kept together, but who would infallibly melt as he advanced southward. Even the electors, assembled in Ratisbon, disregarded his representations; and, influenced by an abject complaisance to Ferdinand, refused him even the title of king. But while they mocked him in Ratisbon and Vienna, in Mecklenburg and Pomerania, one strong town after another fell into his hands.

Notwithstanding this contempt, the Emperor thought it proper to offer to adjust his differences with Sweden by negociation, and for that purpose sent plenipotentiaries to Denmark. But their instructions showed how little he was in earnest in these proposals, for he still continued to refuse to Gustavus the title of king. He hoped by this means to throw on the king of Sweden the odium of being the aggressor, and thereby to ensure the support of the States of the empire. The conference at Dantzic proved, as might be expected, fruitless, and the animosity of both parties was increased to its utmost by an intemperate correspondence.

An imperial general, Torquato Conti, who commanded in Pomerania, had, in the mean time, made a vain attempt to wrest Stettin from the Swedes. The Imperialists were driven out from one place after another; Damm, Stargard, Camin, and Wolgast, soon fell into the hands of Gustavus. To revenge himself upon the Duke of Pomerania, the imperial general permitted his troops, upon his retreat, to exercise every barbarity on the unfortunate inhabitants of Pomerania, who had already suffered but too severely from his avarice. On pretence of cutting off the resources of the Swedes, the whole country was laid waste and plundered; and often when the Imperialists were unable any longer to maintain a place, it was laid in ashes, in order to leave the enemy nothing but ruins. But these barbarities only served to place in a more favourable light the opposite conduct of the Swedes, and to win all hearts to their humane monarch. The Swedish soldier paid for all he required; no private property was injured on his march. The Swedes consequently were received with open arms both in town and country, whilst every Imperialist that fell into the hands of the Pomeranian peasantry was ruthlessly murdered. Many Pomeranians entered into the service of Sweden, and the estates of this exhausted country willingly voted the king a contribution of 100,000 florins.

Torquato Conti, who, with all his severity of character, was a consummate general, endeavoured to render Stettin useless to the king of Sweden, as he could not deprive him of it. He entrenched himself upon the Oder, at Gartz, above Stettin, in order, by commanding that river, to cut off the water communication of the town with the rest of Germany. Nothing could induce him to attack the King of Sweden, who was his superior in numbers, while the latter was equally cautious not to storm the strong entrenchments of the Imperialists. Torquato, too deficient in troops and money to act upon the offensive against the king, hoped by this plan of operations to give time for

Tilly to hasten to the defence of Pomerania, and then, in conjunction with that general, to attack the Swedes. Seizing the opportunity of the temporary absence of Gustavus, he made a sudden attempt upon Stettin, but the Swedes were not unprepared for him. A vigorous attack of the Imperialists was firmly repulsed, and Torquato was forced to retire with great loss. For this auspicious commencement of the war, however, Gustavus was, it must be owned, as much indebted to his good fortune as to his military talents. The imperial troops in Pomerania had been greatly reduced since Wallenstein's dismissal; moreover, the outrages they had committed were now severely revenged upon them; wasted and exhausted, the country no longer afforded them a subsistence. All discipline was at an end; the orders of the officers were disregarded, while their numbers daily decreased by desertion, and by a general mortality, which the piercing cold of a strange climate had produced among them.

Under these circumstances, the imperial general was anxious to allow his troops the repose of winter quarters, but he had to do with an enemy to whom the climate of Germany had no winter. Gustavus had taken the precaution of providing his soldiers with dresses of sheep-skin, to enable them to keep the field even in the most inclement season. The imperial plenipotentiaries, who came to treat with him for a cessation of hostilities, received this discouraging answer: "The Swedes are soldiers in winter as well as in summer, and not disposed to oppress the unfortunate peasantry. The Imperialists may act as they think proper, but they need not expect to remain undisturbed." Torquato Conti soon after resigned a command, in which neither riches nor reputation were to be gained.

In this inequality of the two armies, the advantage was necessarily on the side of the Swedes. The Imperialists were incessantly harassed in their winter quarters; Greifenhagan, an important place upon the Oder, taken by storm, and the towns of Gartz and Piritz were at last abandoned by the enemy. In the whole of Pomerania, Greifswald, Demmin, and Colberg alone remained in their hands, and these the king made great preparations to besiege. The enemy directed their retreat towards Brandenburg, in which much of their artillery and baggage, and many prisoners fell into the hands of the pursuers.

By seizing the passes of Riebnitz and Damgarden, Gustavus had opened a passage into Mecklenburg, whose inhabitants were invited to return to their allegiance under their legitimate sovereigns, and to expel the adherents of Wallenstein. The Imperialists, however, gained the important town of Rostock by stratagem, and thus prevented the farther advance of the king, who was unwilling to divide his forces. The exiled dukes of Mecklenburg had ineffectually employed the princes assembled at Ratisbon to intercede with the Emperor: in vain they had endeavoured to soften Ferdinand, by renouncing the alliance of the king, and every idea of resistance. But, driven to despair by the Emperor's inflexibility, they openly espoused the side of Sweden, and raising troops, gave the command of them to Francis Charles Duke of Saxe-Lauenburg. That general made himself master of several strong places on the Elbe, but lost them afterwards to the Imperial General Pappenheim, who was despatched to oppose him. Soon afterwards, besieged by the latter in the town of Ratzeburg, he was compelled to surrender with all his troops. Thus ended the attempt which these unfortunate princes made to recover their territories; and it was reserved for the victorious arm of Gustavus Adolphus to render them that brilliant service.

The Imperialists had thrown themselves into Brandenburg, which now became the theatre of the most barbarous atrocities. These outrages were inflicted upon the subjects of a prince who had never injured the Emperor, and whom, moreover, he was at the very time inciting to take up arms against the King of Sweden. The sight of the disorders of their soldiers, which want of money compelled them to wink at, and of authority over their troops, excited the disgust even of the imperial generals; and, from very shame, their commander-in-chief, Count Schaumburg, wished to resign.

Without a sufficient force to protect his territories, and left by the Emperor, in spite of the most pressing remonstrances, without assistance, the Elector of Brandenburg at last issued an edict, ordering his subjects to repel force by force, and to put to death without mercy every Imperial soldier who should henceforth be detected in plundering. To such a height had the violence of outrage and the misery of the government risen, that nothing was left to the sovereign, but the desperate extremity of sanctioning private vengeance by a formal law.

The Swedes had pursued the Imperialists into Brandenburg; and only the Elector's refusal to open to him the fortress of Custrin for his march, obliged the king to lay aside his design of besieging Frankfort on the Oder. He therefore returned to complete the conquest of Pomerania, by the capture of Demmin and Colberg. In the mean time, Field-Marshal Tilly was advancing to the defence of Brandenburg.

This general, who could boast as yet of never having suffered a defeat, the conqueror of Mansfeld, of Duke Christian of Brunswick, of the Margrave of Baden, and the King of Denmark, was now in the Swedish monarch to meet an opponent worthy of his fame. Descended of a noble family in Liege, Tilly had formed his military talents in the wars of the Netherlands, which was then the great school for generals. He soon found an opportunity of distinguishing himself under Rodolph II. in Hungary, where he rapidly rose from one step to another. After the peace, he entered into the service of Maximilian of Bavaria, who made him commander-in-chief with absolute powers. Here, by his excellent regulations, he was the founder of the Bavarian army; and to him, chiefly, Maximilian was indebted for his superiority in the field. Upon the termination of the Bohemian war, he was appointed commander of the troops of the League; and, after Wallenstein's dismissal, generalissimo of the imperial armies. Equally stern towards his soldiers and implacable towards his enemies, and as gloomy and impenetrable as Wallenstein, he was greatly his superior in probity and disinterestedness. A bigoted zeal for religion, and a bloody spirit of persecution, co-operated, with the natural ferocity of his character, to make him the terror of the Protestants. A strange and terrific aspect bespoke his character: of low stature, thin, with hollow cheeks, a long nose, a broad and wrinkled forehead, large whiskers, and a pointed chin; he was generally attired in a Spanish doublet of green satin, with slashed sleeves, with a small high peaked hat upon his head, surmounted by a red feather which hung down to his back. His whole aspect recalled to recollection the Duke of Alva, the scourge of the Flemings, and his actions were far from effacing the impression. Such was the general who was now to be opposed to the hero of the north.

Tilly was far from undervaluing his antagonist, "The King of Sweden," said he in the Diet at Ratisbon, "is an enemy both prudent and brave, inured to war, and in the flower of his age. His plans are excellent, his resources considerable; his subjects enthusiastically attached to him. His army, composed of Swedes, Germans, Livonians, Finlanders, Scots and English, by its devoted obedience to their leader, is blended into one nation: he is a gamester in playing with whom not to have lost is to have won a great deal."

The progress of the King of Sweden in Brandenburg and Pomerania, left the new generalissimo no time to lose; and his presence was now urgently called for by those who commanded in that quarter. With all expedition, he collected the imperial troops which were dispersed over the empire; but it required time to obtain from the exhausted and impoverished provinces the necessary supplies. At last, about the middle of winter, he appeared at the head of 20,000 men, before Frankfort on the Oder, where he was joined by Schaumburg. Leaving to this general the defence of Frankfort, with a sufficient garrison, he hastened to Pomerania, with a view of saving Demmin, and relieving Colberg, which was already hard pressed by the Swedes. But even before he had left Brandenburg, Demmin, which was but poorly defended by the Duke of Savelli, had surrendered to the king, and Colberg, after a five months' siege, was starved into a capitulation. As the passes in Upper Pomerania were well guarded, and the king's camp near Schwedt defied attack, Tilly abandoned his offensive plan of operations, and retreated towards the Elbe to besiege Magdeburg.

The capture of Demmin opened to the king a free passage into Mecklenburg; but a more important enterprise drew his arms into another quarter. Scarcely had Tilly commenced his retrograde movement, when suddenly breaking up his camp at Schwedt, the king marched his whole force against Frankfort on the Oder. This town, badly fortified, was defended by a garrison of 8,000 men, mostly composed of those ferocious bands who had so cruelly ravaged Pomerania and Brandenburg. It was now attacked with such impetuosity, that on the third day it was taken by storm. The Swedes, assured of victory, rejected every offer of capitulation, as they were resolved to exercise the dreadful right of retaliation. For Tilly, soon after his arrival, had surrounded a Swedish detachment, and, irritated by their obstinate resistance, had cut them in pieces to a man. This cruelty was not forgotten by the Swedes. "New Brandenburg Quarter", they replied to the Imperialists who begged their lives, and slaughtered them without mercy. Several thousands were either killed or taken, and many were drowned in the Oder, the rest fled to Silesia. All their artillery fell into the hands of the Swedes. To satisfy the rage of his troops, Gustavus Adolphus was under the necessity of giving up the town for three hours to plunder.

While the king was thus advancing from one conquest to another, and, by his success, encouraging the Protestants to active resistance, the Emperor proceeded to enforce the Edict of Restitution, and, by his exorbitant pretensions, to exhaust the patience of the states. Compelled by necessity, he continued the violent course which he had begun with such arrogant confidence; the difficulties into which his arbitrary conduct had plunged him, he could only extricate himself from by measures still more arbitrary. But in so complicated a body as the German empire, despotism must always create the most dangerous convulsions. With astonishment, the princes beheld the constitution of the empire overthrown, and the state of nature to which matters were again verging, suggested to them the idea of self-defence, the only means of protection in such a state of things. The steps openly taken by the Emperor against the Lutheran church, had at last removed the veil from the eyes of John George, who had been so long the dupe of his artful policy. Ferdinand, too, had personally offended him by the exclusion of his son from the archbishopric of Magdeburg; and field-marshal Arnheim, his new favourite and minister, spared no pains to increase the resentment of his master. Arnheim had formerly been an imperial general under Wallenstein, and being still zealously attached to him, he was eager to avenge his old benefactor and himself on the Emperor, by detaching Saxony from the Austrian interests. Gustavus Adolphus, supported by the Protestant states, would be invincible; a consideration which already filled the Emperor with alarm. The example of Saxony would probably influence others, and the Emperor's fate seemed now in a manner to depend upon the Elector's decision. The artful favourite impressed upon his master this idea of his own importance, and advised him to terrify the Emperor, by threatening an alliance with Sweden, and thus to extort from his fears, what he had sought in vain from his gratitude. The favourite, however, was far from wishing him actually to enter into the Swedish alliance, but, by holding aloof from both parties, to maintain his own importance and independence. Accordingly, he laid before him a plan, which only wanted a more able hand to carry it into execution, and recommended him, by heading the Protestant party, to erect a third power in Germany, and thereby maintain the balance between Sweden and Austria.

This project was peculiarly flattering to the Saxon Elector, to whom the idea of being dependent upon Sweden, or of longer submitting to the tyranny of the Emperor, was equally hateful. He could not, with indifference, see the control of German affairs wrested from him by a foreign prince; and incapable as he was of taking a principal part, his vanity would not condescend to act a subordinate one. He resolved, therefore, to draw every possible advantage from the progress of Gustavus, but to pursue, independently, his own separate plans. With this view, he consulted with the Elector of Brandenburg, who, from similar causes, was ready to act against the Emperor, but, at the same time, was jealous of Sweden. In a Diet at Torgau, having assured himself of the support of his Estates, he invited the Protestant States of the empire to a general convention, which took place at Leipzig, on the 6th February 1631. Brandenburg, Hesse Cassel, with several princes, counts, estates of the empire, and Protestant bishops were present, either personally or by deputy, at this assembly, which the chaplain to the Saxon Court, Dr. Hoe von Hohenegg, opened with a vehement discourse from the pulpit. The Emperor had, in vain, endeavoured to prevent this self-appointed convention, whose object was evidently to provide for its own defence, and which the presence of the Swedes in the empire, rendered more than usually alarming. Emboldened by the progress of Gustavus Adolphus, the assembled princes asserted their rights, and after a session of two months broke up, with adopting a resolution which placed the Emperor in no slight embarrassment. Its import was to demand of the Emperor, in a general address, the revocation of the Edict of Restitution, the withdrawal of his troops from their capitals and fortresses, the suspension of all existing proceedings, and the abolition of abuses; and, in the mean time, to raise an army of 40,000 men, to enable them to redress their own grievances, if the Emperor should still refuse satisfaction.

A further incident contributed not a little to increase the firmness of the Protestant princes. The King of Sweden had, at last, overcome the scruples which had deterred him from a closer alliance with France, and, on the 13th January 1631, concluded a formal treaty with this crown. After a serious dispute respecting the treatment of the Roman Catholic princes of the empire, whom France took under her protection, and against whom Gustavus claimed the right of retaliation, and after some less important differences with regard to the title of majesty, which the pride of France was loth to concede to the King of Sweden, Richelieu yielded the second, and Gustavus Adolphus the first point, and the treaty was signed at Beerwald in Neumark. The contracting parties mutually covenanted to defend each other with a military force, to protect their common friends, to restore to their dominions the deposed princes of the empire, and to replace every thing, both on the frontier and in the interior of Germany, on the same footing on which it stood before the commencement of the war. For this end, Sweden engaged to maintain an army of 30,000 men in Germany, and France agreed to furnish the Swedes with an annual subsidy of 400,000 dollars. If the arms of Gustavus were successful, he was to respect the Roman Catholic religion and the constitution of the empire in all the conquered places, and to make no attempt against either. All Estates and princes whether Protestant or Roman Catholic, either in Germany or in other countries, were to be invited to become parties to the treaty; neither France nor Sweden was to conclude a separate peace without the knowledge and consent of the other; and the treaty itself was to continue in force for five years.

Great as was the struggle to the King of Sweden to receive subsidies from France, and sacrifice his independence in the conduct of the war, this alliance with France decided his cause in Germany. Protected, as he now was, by the greatest power in Europe, the German states began to feel confidence in his undertaking, for the issue of which they had hitherto good reason to tremble. He became truly formidable to the Emperor. The Roman Catholic princes too, who, though they were anxious to humble Austria, had witnessed his progress with distrust, were less alarmed now that an alliance with a Roman Catholic power ensured his respect for their religion. And thus, while Gustavus Adolphus protected the Protestant religion and the liberties of Germany against the aggression of Ferdinand, France secured those liberties, and the Roman Catholic religion, against Gustavus himself, if the intoxication of success should hurry him beyond the bounds of moderation.

The King of Sweden lost no time in apprizing the members of the confederacy of Leipzig of the treaty concluded with France, and inviting them to a closer union with himself. The application was seconded by France, who spared no pains to win over the Elector of Saxony. Gustavus was willing to be content with secret support, if the princes should deem it too bold a step as yet to declare openly in his favour. Several princes gave him hopes of his proposals being accepted on the first favourable opportunity; but the Saxon Elector, full of jealousy and distrust towards the King of Sweden, and true to the selfish policy he had pursued, could not be prevailed upon to give a decisive answer.

The resolution of the confederacy of Leipzig, and the alliance betwixt France and Sweden, were news equally disagreeable to the Emperor. Against them he employed the thunder of imperial ordinances, and the want of an army saved France from the full weight of his displeasure. Remonstrances were addressed to all the members of the confederacy, strongly prohibiting them from enlisting troops. They retorted with explanations equally vehement, justified their conduct upon the principles of natural right, and continued their preparations.

Meantime, the imperial generals, deficient both in troops and money, found themselves reduced to the disagreeable alternative of losing sight either of the King of Sweden, or of the Estates of the empire, since with a divided force they were not a match for either. The movements of the Protestants called their attention to the interior of the empire, while the progress of the king in Brandenburg, by threatening the hereditary possessions of Austria, required them to turn their arms to that quarter. After the conquest of Frankfort, the king had advanced upon Landsberg on the Warta, and Tilly, after a fruitless attempt to relieve it, had again returned to Magdeburg, to prosecute with vigour the siege of that town.

The rich archbishopric, of which Magdeburg was the capital, had long been in the possession of princes of the house of Brandenburg, who introduced the Protestant religion into the province. Christian William, the last administrator, had, by his alliance with Denmark, incurred the ban of the empire, on which account the chapter, to avoid the Emperor's displeasure, had formally deposed him. In his place they had elected Prince John Augustus, the second son of the Elector of Saxony, whom the Emperor rejected, in order to confer the archbishopric on his son Leopold. The Elector of Saxony complained ineffectually to the imperial court; but Christian William of Brandenburg took more active measures. Relying on the attachment of the magistracy and inhabitants of Brandenburg, and excited by chimerical hopes, he thought himself able to surmount all the obstacles which the vote of the chapter, the competition of two powerful rivals, and the Edict of Restitution opposed to his restoration. He went to Sweden, and, by the promise of a diversion in Germany, sought to obtain assistance from Gustavus. He was dismissed by that monarch not without hopes of effectual protection, but with the advice to act with caution.

Scarcely had Christian William been informed of the landing of his protector in Pomerania, than he entered Magdeburg in disguise. Appearing suddenly in the town council, he reminded the magistrates of the ravages which both town and country had suffered from the imperial troops, of the pernicious designs of Ferdinand, and the danger of the Protestant church. He then informed them that the moment of deliverance was at hand, and that Gustavus Adolphus offered them his alliance and assistance. Magdeburg, one of the most flourishing towns in Germany, enjoyed under the government of its magistrates a republican freedom, which inspired its citizens with a brave heroism. Of this they had already given proofs, in the bold defence of their rights against Wallenstein, who, tempted by their wealth, made on them the most extravagant demands. Their territory had been given up to the fury of his troops, though Magdeburg itself had escaped his vengeance. It was not difficult, therefore, for the Administrator to gain the concurrence of men in whose minds the rememberance of these outrages was still recent. An alliance was formed between the city and the Swedish king, by which Magdeburg granted to the king a free passage through its gates and territories, with liberty of enlisting soldiers within its boundaries, and on the other hand, obtained promises of effectual protection for its religion and its privileges.

The Administrator immediately collected troops and commenced hostilities, before Gustavus Adolphus was near enough to co-operate with him. He defeated some imperial detachments in the neighbourhood, made a few conquests, and even surprised Halle. But the approach of an imperial army obliged him to retreat hastily, and not without loss, to Magdeburg. Gustavus Adolphus, though displeased with his premature measures, sent Dietrich Falkenberg, an experienced officer, to direct the Administrator's military operations, and to assist him with his counsel. Falkenberg was named by the magistrates governor of the town during the war. The Prince's army was daily augmented by recruits from the neighbouring towns; and he was able for some months to maintain a petty warfare with success.

At length Count Pappenheim, having brought his expedition against the Duke of Saxe-Lauenburg to a close, approached the town. Driving the troops of the Administrator from their entrenchments, he cut off his communication with Saxony, and closely invested the place. He was soon followed by Tilly, who haughtily summoned the Elector forthwith to comply with the Edict of Restitution, to submit to the Emperor's orders, and surrender Magdeburg. The Prince's answer was spirited and resolute, and obliged Tilly at once to have recourse to arms.

In the meanwhile, the siege was prolonged, by the progress of the King of Sweden, which called the Austrian general from before the place; and the jealousy of the officers, who conducted the operations in his absence, delayed, for some months, the fall of Magdeburg. On the 30th March 1631, Tilly returned, to push the siege with vigour.

The outworks were soon carried, and Falkenberg, after withdrawing the garrisons from the points which he could no longer hold, destroyed the bridge over the Elbe. As his troops were barely sufficient to defend the extensive fortifications, the suburbs of Sudenburg and Neustadt were abandoned to the enemy, who immediately laid them in ashes. Pappenheim, now separated from Tilly, crossed the Elbe at Schonenbeck, and attacked the town from the opposite side.

The garrison, reduced by the defence of the outworks, scarcely exceeded 2000 infantry and a few hundred horse; a small number for so extensive and irregular a fortress. To supply this deficiency, the citizens were armed—a desperate expedient, which produced more evils than those it prevented. The citizens, at best but indifferent soldiers, by their disunion threw the town into confusion. The poor complained that they were exposed to every hardship and danger, while the rich, by hiring substitutes, remained at home in safety. These rumours broke out at last in an open mutiny; indifference succeeded to zeal; weariness and negligence took the place of vigilance and foresight. Dissension, combined with growing scarcity, gradually produced a feeling of despondence, many began to tremble at the desperate nature of their undertaking, and the magnitude of the power to which they were opposed. But religious zeal, an ardent love of liberty, an invincible hatred to the Austrian yoke, and the expectation of speedy relief, banished as yet the idea of a surrender; and divided as they were in every thing else, they were united in the resolve to defend themselves to the last extremity.

Their hopes of succour were apparently well founded. They knew that the confederacy of Leipzig was arming; they were aware of the near approach of Gustavus Adolphus. Both were alike interested in the preservation of Magdeburg; and a few days might bring the King of Sweden before its walls. All this was also known to Tilly, who, therefore, was anxious to make himself speedily master of the place. With this view, he had despatched a trumpeter with letters to the Administrator, the commandant, and the magistrates, offering terms of capitulation; but he received for answer, that they would rather die than surrender. A spirited sally of the citizens, also convinced him that their courage was as earnest as their words, while the king's arrival at Potsdam, with the incursions of the Swedes as far as Zerbst, filled him with uneasiness, but raised the hopes of the garrison. A second trumpeter was now despatched; but the more moderate tone of his demands increased the confidence of the besieged, and unfortunately their negligence also.

The besiegers had now pushed their approaches as far as the ditch, and vigorously cannonaded the fortifications from the abandoned batteries. One tower was entirely overthrown, but this did not facilitate an assault, as it fell sidewise upon the wall, and not into the ditch. Notwithstanding the continual bombardment, the walls had not suffered much; and the fire balls, which were intended to set the town in flames, were deprived of their effect by the excellent precautions adopted against them. But the ammunition of the besieged was nearly expended, and the cannon of the town gradually ceased to answer the fire of the Imperialists. Before a new supply could be obtained, Magdeburg would be either relieved, or taken. The hopes of the besieged were on the stretch, and all eyes anxiously directed towards the quarter in which the Swedish banners were expected to appear. Gustavus Adolphus was near enough to reach Magdeburg within three days; security grew with hope, which all things contributed to augment. On the 9th of May, the fire of the Imperialists was suddenly stopped, and the cannon withdrawn from several of the batteries. A deathlike stillness reigned in the Imperial camp. The besieged were convinced that deliverance was at hand. Both citizens and soldiers left their posts upon the ramparts early in the morning, to indulge themselves, after their long toils, with the refreshment of sleep, but it was indeed a dear sleep, and a frightful awakening.

Tilly had abandoned the hope of taking the town, before the arrival of the Swedes, by the means which he had hitherto adopted; he therefore determined to raise the siege, but first to hazard a general assault. This plan, however, was attended with great difficulties, as no breach had been effected, and the works were scarcely injured. But the council of war assembled on this occasion, declared for an assault, citing the example of Maestricht, which had been taken early in the morning, while the citizens and soldiers were reposing themselves. The attack was to be made simultaneously on four points; the night betwixt the 9th and 10th of May, was employed in the necessary preparations. Every thing was ready and awaiting the signal, which was to be given by cannon at five o'clock in the morning. The signal, however, was not given for two hours later, during which Tilly, who was still doubtful of success, again consulted the council of war. Pappenheim was ordered to attack the works of the new town, where the attempt was favoured by a sloping rampart, and a dry ditch of moderate depth. The citizens and soldiers had mostly left the walls, and the few who remained were overcome with sleep. This general, therefore, found little difficulty in mounting the wall at the head of his troops.

Falkenberg, roused by the report of musketry, hastened from the town-house, where he was employed in despatching Tilly's second trumpeter, and hurried with all the force he could hastily assemble towards the gate of the new town, which was already in the possession of the enemy. Beaten back, this intrepid general flew to another quarter, where a second party of the enemy were preparing to scale the walls. After an ineffectual resistance he fell in the commencement of the action. The roaring of musketry, the pealing of the alarm-bells, and the growing tumult apprised the awakening citizens of their danger. Hastily arming themselves, they rushed in blind confusion against the enemy. Still some hope of repulsing the besiegers remained; but the governor being killed, their efforts were without plan and co-operation, and at last their ammunition began to fail them. In the meanwhile, two other gates, hitherto unattacked, were stripped of their defenders, to meet the urgent danger within the town. The enemy quickly availed themselves of this confusion to attack these posts. The resistance was nevertheless spirited and obstinate, until four imperial regiments, at length, masters of the ramparts, fell upon the garrison in the rear, and completed their rout. Amidst the general tumult, a brave captain, named Schmidt, who still headed a few of the more resolute against the enemy, succeeded in driving them to the gates; here he fell mortally wounded, and with him expired the hopes of Magdeburg. Before noon, all the works were carried, and the town was in the enemy's hands.

Two gates were now opened by the storming party for the main body, and Tilly marched in with part of his infantry. Immediately occupying the principal streets, he drove the citizens with pointed cannon into their dwellings, there to await their destiny. They were not long held in suspense; a word from Tilly decided the fate of Magdeburg.

Even a more humane general would in vain have recommended mercy to such soldiers; but Tilly never made the attempt. Left by their general's silence masters of the lives of all the citizens, the soldiery broke into the houses to satiate their most brutal appetites. The prayers of innocence excited some compassion in the hearts of the Germans, but none in the rude breasts of Pappenheim's Walloons. Scarcely had the savage cruelty commenced, when the other gates were thrown open, and the cavalry, with the fearful hordes of the Croats, poured in upon the devoted inhabitants.

Here commenced a scene of horrors for which history has no language— poetry no pencil. Neither innocent childhood, nor helpless old age; neither youth, sex, rank, nor beauty, could disarm the fury of the conquerors. Wives were abused in the arms of their husbands, daughters at the feet of their parents; and the defenceless sex exposed to the double sacrifice of virtue and life. No situation, however obscure, or however sacred, escaped the rapacity of the enemy. In a single church fifty-three women were found beheaded. The Croats amused themselves with throwing children into the flames; Pappenheim's Walloons with stabbing infants at the mother's breast. Some officers of the League, horror-struck at this dreadful scene, ventured to remind Tilly that he had it in his power to stop the carnage. "Return in an hour," was his answer; "I will see what I can do; the soldier must have some reward for his danger and toils." These horrors lasted with unabated fury, till at last the smoke and flames proved a check to the plunderers. To augment the confusion and to divert the resistance of the inhabitants, the Imperialists had, in the commencement of the assault, fired the town in several places. The wind rising rapidly, spread the flames, till the blaze became universal. Fearful, indeed, was the tumult amid clouds of smoke, heaps of dead bodies, the clash of swords, the crash of falling ruins, and streams of blood. The atmosphere glowed; and the intolerable heat forced at last even the murderers to take refuge in their camp. In less than twelve hours, this strong, populous, and flourishing city, one of the finest in Germany, was reduced to ashes, with the exception of two churches and a few houses. The Administrator,

Christian William, after receiving several wounds, was taken prisoner, with three of the burgomasters; most of the officers and magistrates had already met an enviable death. The avarice of the officers had saved 400 of the richest citizens, in the hope of extorting from them an exorbitant ransom. But this humanity was confined to the officers of the League, whom the ruthless barbarity of the Imperialists caused to be regarded as guardian angels.

Scarcely had the fury of the flames abated, when the Imperialists returned to renew the pillage amid the ruins and ashes of the town. Many were suffocated by the smoke; many found rich booty in the cellars, where the citizens had concealed their more valuable effects. On the 13th of May, Tilly himself appeared in the town, after the streets had been cleared of ashes and dead bodies. Horrible and revolting to humanity was the scene that presented itself. The living crawling from under the dead, children wandering about with heart-rending cries, calling for their parents; and infants still sucking the breasts of their lifeless mothers. More than 6,000 bodies were thrown into the Elbe to clear the streets; a much greater number had been consumed by the flames. The whole number of the slain was reckoned at not less than 30,000.

The entrance of the general, which took place on the 14th, put a stop to the plunder, and saved the few who had hitherto contrived to escape. About a thousand people were taken out of the cathedral, where they had remained three days and two nights, without food, and in momentary fear of death. Tilly promised them quarter, and commanded bread to be distributed among them. The next day, a solemn mass was performed in the cathedral, and 'Te Deum' sung amidst the discharge of artillery. The imperial general rode through the streets, that he might be able, as an eyewitness, to inform his master that no such conquest had been made since the destruction of Troy and Jerusalem. Nor was this an exaggeration, whether we consider the greatness, importance, and prosperity of the city razed, or the fury of its ravagers.

In Germany, the tidings of the dreadful fate of Magdeburg caused triumphant joy to the Roman Catholics, while it spread terror and consternation among the Protestants. Loudly and generally they complained against the king of Sweden, who, with so strong a force, and in the very neighbourhood, had left an allied city to its fate. Even the most reasonable deemed his inaction inexplicable; and lest he should lose irretrievably the good will of the people, for whose deliverance he had engaged in this war, Gustavus was under the necessity of publishing to the world a justification of his own conduct.

He had attacked, and on the 16th April, carried Landsberg, when he was apprised of the danger of Magdeburg. He resolved immediately to march to the relief of that town; and he moved with all his cavalry, and ten regiments of infantry towards the Spree. But the position which he held in Germany, made it necessary that he should not move forward without securing his rear. In traversing a country where he was surrounded by suspicious friends and dangerous enemies, and where a single premature movement might cut off his communication with his own kingdom, the utmost vigilance and caution were necessary. The Elector of Brandenburg had already opened the fortress of Custrin to the flying Imperialists, and closed the gates against their pursuers. If now Gustavus should fail in his attack upon Tilly, the Elector might again open his fortresses to the Imperialists, and the king, with an enemy both in front and rear, would be irrecoverably lost. In order to prevent this contingency, he demanded that the Elector should allow him to hold the fortresses of Custrin and Spandau, till the siege of Magdeburg should be raised.

Nothing could be more reasonable than this demand. The services which Gustavus had lately rendered the Elector, by expelling the Imperialists from Brandenburg, claimed his gratitude, while the past conduct of the Swedes in Germany entitled them to confidence. But by the surrender of his fortresses, the Elector would in some measure make the King of Sweden master of his country; besides that, by such a step, he must at once break with the Emperor, and expose his States to his future vengeance. The Elector's struggle with himself was long and violent, but pusillanimity and self-interest for awhile prevailed. Unmoved by the fate of Magdeburg, cold in the cause of religion and the liberties of Germany, he saw nothing but his own danger; and this anxiety was greatly stimulated by his minister Von Schwartzenburgh, who was secretly in the pay of Austria. In the mean time, the Swedish troops approached Berlin, and the king took up his residence with the Elector. When he witnessed the timorous hesitation of that prince, he could not restrain his indignation: "My road is to Magdeburg," said he; "not for my own advantage, but for that of the Protestant religion. If no one will stand by me, I shall immediately retreat, conclude a peace with the Emperor, and return to Stockholm. I am convinced that Ferdinand will readily grant me whatever conditions I may require. But if Magdeburg is once lost, and the Emperor relieved from all fear of me, then it is for you to look to yourselves and the consequences." This timely threat, and perhaps, too, the aspect of the Swedish army, which was strong enough to obtain by force what was refused to entreaty, brought at last the Elector to his senses, and Spandau was delivered into the hands of the Swedes.

The king had now two routes to Magdeburg; one westward led through an exhausted country, and filled with the enemy's troops, who might dispute with him the passage of the Elbe; the other more to the southward, by Dessau and Wittenberg, where bridges were to be found for crossing the Elbe, and where supplies could easily be drawn from Saxony. But he could not avail himself of the latter without the consent of the Elector, whom Gustavus had good reason to distrust. Before setting out on his march, therefore, he demanded from that prince a free passage and liberty for purchasing provisions for his troops. His application was refused, and no remonstrances could prevail on the Elector to abandon his system of neutrality. While the point was still in dispute, the news of the dreadful fate of Magdeburg arrived.

Tilly announced its fall to the Protestant princes in the tone of a conqueror, and lost no time in making the most of the general consternation. The influence of the Emperor, which had sensibly declined during the rapid progress of Gustavus, after this decisive blow rose higher than ever; and the change was speedily visible in the imperious tone he adopted towards the Protestant states. The decrees of the Confederation of Leipzig were annulled by a proclamation, the Convention itself suppressed by an imperial decree, and all the refractory states threatened with the fate of Magdeburg. As the executor of this imperial mandate, Tilly immediately ordered troops to march against the Bishop of Bremen, who was a member of the Confederacy, and had himself enlisted soldiers. The terrified bishop immediately gave up his forces to Tilly, and signed the revocation of the acts of the Confederation. An imperial army, which had lately returned from Italy, under the command of Count Furstenberg, acted in the same manner towards the Administrator of Wirtemberg. The duke was compelled to submit to the Edict of Restitution, and all the decrees of the Emperor, and even to pay a monthly subsidy of 100,000 dollars, for the maintenance of the imperial troops. Similar burdens were inflicted upon Ulm and Nuremberg, and the entire circles of Franconia and Swabia. The hand of the Emperor was stretched in terror over all Germany. The sudden preponderance, more in appearance, perhaps, than in reality, which he had obtained by this blow, carried him beyond the bounds even of the moderation which he had hitherto observed, and misled him into hasty and violent measures, which at last turned the wavering resolution of the German princes in favour of Gustavus Adolphus. Injurious as the immediate consequences of the fall of Magdeburg were to the Protestant cause, its remoter effects were most advantageous. The past surprise made way for active resentment, despair inspired courage, and the German freedom rose, like a phoenix, from the ashes of Magdeburg.

Among the princes of the Leipzig Confederation, the Elector of Saxony and the Landgrave of Hesse were the most powerful; and, until they were disarmed, the universal authority of the Emperor was unconfirmed. Against the Landgrave, therefore, Tilly first directed his attack, and marched straight from Magdeburg into Thuringia. During this march, the territories of Saxe Ernest and Schwartzburg were laid waste, and Frankenhausen plundered before the very eyes of Tilly, and laid in ashes with impunity. The unfortunate peasant paid dear for his master's attachment to the interests of Sweden.

Erfurt, the key of Saxony and Franconia, was threatened with a siege, but redeemed itself by a voluntary contribution of money and provisions. From thence, Tilly despatched his emissaries to the Landgrave, demanding of him the immediate disbanding of his army, a renunciation of the league of Leipzig, the reception of imperial garrisons into his territories and fortresses, with the necessary contributions, and the declaration of friendship or hostility. Such was the treatment which a prince of the Empire was compelled to submit to from a servant of the Emperor. But these extravagant demands acquired a formidable weight from the power which supported them; and the dreadful fate of Magdeburg, still fresh in the memory of the Landgrave, tended still farther to enforce them. Admirable, therefore, was the intrepidity of the Landgrave's answer: "To admit foreign troops into his capital and fortresses, the Landgrave is not disposed; his troops he requires for his own purposes; as for an attack, he can defend himself. If General Tilly wants money or provisions, let him go to Munich, where there is plenty of both." The irruption of two bodies of imperial troops into Hesse Cassel was the immediate result of this spirited reply, but the Landgrave gave them so warm a reception that they could effect nothing; and just as Tilly was preparing to follow with his whole army, to punish the unfortunate country for the firmness of its sovereign, the movements of the King of Sweden recalled him to another quarter.

Gustavus Adolphus had learned the fall of Magdeburg with deep regret; and the demand now made by the Elector, George William, in terms of their agreement, for the restoration of Spandau, greatly increased this feeling. The loss of Magdeburg had rather augmented than lessened the reasons which made the possession of this fortress so desirable; and the nearer became the necessity of a decisive battle between himself and Tilly, the more unwilling he felt to abandon the only place which, in the event of a defeat, could ensure him a refuge. After a vain endeavour, by entreaties and representations, to bring over the Elector to his views, whose coldness and lukewarmness daily increased, he gave orders to his general to evacuate Spandau, but at the same time declared to the Elector that he would henceforth regard him as an enemy.

To give weight to this declaration, he appeared with his whole force before Berlin. "I will not be worse treated than the imperial generals," was his reply to the ambassadors whom the bewildered Elector despatched to his camp. "Your master has received them into his territories, furnished them with all necessary supplies, ceded to them every place which they required, and yet, by all these concessions, he could not prevail upon them to treat his subjects with common humanity. All that I require of him is security, a moderate sum of money, and provisions for my troops; in return, I promise to protect his country, and to keep the war at a distance from him. On these points, however, I must insist; and my brother, the Elector, must instantly determine to have me as a friend, or to see his capital plundered." This decisive tone produced a due impression; and the cannon pointed against the town put an end to the doubts of George William. In a few days, a treaty was signed, by which the Elector engaged to furnish a monthly subsidy of 30,000 dollars, to leave Spandau in the king's hands, and to open Custrin at all times to the Swedish troops. This now open alliance of the Elector of Brandenburg with the Swedes, excited no less displeasure at Vienna, than did formerly the similar procedure of the Duke of Pomerania; but the changed fortune which now attended his arms, obliged the Emperor to confine his resentment to words.

The king's satisfaction, on this favourable event, was increased by the agreeable intelligence that Griefswald, the only fortress which the Imperialists still held in Pomerania, had surrendered, and that the whole country was now free of the enemy. He appeared once more in this duchy, and was gratified at the sight of the general joy which he had caused to the people. A year had elapsed since Gustavus first entered Germany, and this event was now celebrated by all Pomerania as a national festival. Shortly before, the Czar of Moscow had sent ambassadors to congratulate him, to renew his alliance, and even to offer him troops. He had great reason to rejoice at the friendly disposition of Russia, as it was indispensable to his interests that Sweden itself should remain undisturbed by any dangerous neighbour during the war in which he himself was engaged. Soon after, his queen, Maria Eleonora, landed in Pomerania, with a reinforcement of 8000 Swedes; and the arrival of 6000 English, under the Marquis of Hamilton, requires more particular notice because this is all that history mentions of the English during the Thirty Years' War.

During Tilly's expedition into Thuringia, Pappenheim commanded in Magdeburg; but was unable to prevent the Swedes from crossing the Elbe at various points, routing some imperial detachments, and seizing several posts. He himself, alarmed at the approach of the King of Sweden, anxiously recalled Tilly, and prevailed upon him to return by rapid marches to Magdeburg. Tilly encamped on this side of the river at Wolmerstadt; Gustavus on the same side, near Werben, not far from the confluence of the Havel and the Elbe. His very arrival portended no good to Tilly. The Swedes routed three of his regiments, which were posted in villages at some distance from the main body, carried off half their baggage, and burned the remainder. Tilly in vain advanced within cannon shot of the king's camp, and offered him battle. Gustavus, weaker by one-half than his adversary, prudently declined it; and his position was too strong for an attack. Nothing more ensued but a distant cannonade, and a few skirmishes, in which the Swedes had invariably the advantage. In his retreat to Wolmerstadt, Tilly's army was weakened by numerous desertions. Fortune seemed to have forsaken him since the carnage of Magdeburg.

The King of Sweden, on the contrary, was followed by uninterrupted success. While he himself was encamped in Werben, the whole of Mecklenburg, with the exception of a few towns, was conquered by his General Tott and the Duke Adolphus Frederick; and he enjoyed the satisfaction of reinstating both dukes in their dominions. He proceeded in person to Gustrow, where the reinstatement was solemnly to take place, to give additional dignity to the ceremony by his presence. The two dukes, with their deliverer between them, and attended by a splendid train of princes, made a public entry into the city, which the joy of their subjects converted into an affecting solemnity. Soon after his return to Werben, the Landgrave of Hesse Cassel appeared in his camp, to conclude an offensive and defensive alliance; the first sovereign prince in Germany, who voluntarily and openly declared against the Emperor, though not wholly uninfluenced by strong motives. The Landgrave bound himself to act against the king's enemies as his own, to open to him his towns and territory, and to furnish his army with provisions and necessaries. The king, on the other hand, declared himself his ally and protector; and engaged to conclude no peace with the Emperor without first obtaining for the Landgrave a full redress of grievances. Both parties honourably performed their agreement. Hesse Cassel adhered to the Swedish alliance during the whole of this tedious war; and at the peace of Westphalia had no reason to regret the friendship of Sweden.

Tilly, from whom this bold step on the part of the Landgrave was not long concealed, despatched Count Fugger with several regiments against him; and at the same time endeavoured to excite his subjects to rebellion by inflammatory letters. But these made as little impression as his troops, which subsequently failed him so decidedly at the battle of Breitenfeld. The Estates of Hesse could not for a moment hesitate between their oppressor and their protector.

But the imperial general was far more disturbed by the equivocal conduct of the Elector of Saxony, who, in defiance of the imperial prohibition, continued his preparations, and adhered to the confederation of Leipzig. At this conjuncture, when the proximity of the King of Sweden made a decisive battle ere long inevitable, it appeared extremely dangerous to leave Saxony in arms, and ready in a moment to declare for the enemy. Tilly had just received a reinforcement of 25,000 veteran troops under Furstenberg, and, confident in his strength, he hoped either to disarm the Elector by the mere terror of his arrival, or at least to conquer him with little difficulty. Before quitting his camp at Wolmerstadt, he commanded the Elector, by a special messenger, to open his territories to the imperial troops; either to disband his own, or to join them to the imperial army; and to assist, in conjunction with himself, in driving the King of Sweden out of Germany. While he reminded him that, of all the German states, Saxony had hitherto been most respected, he threatened it, in case of refusal, with the most destructive ravages.

But Tilly had chosen an unfavourable moment for so imperious a requisition. The ill-treatment of his religious and political confederates, the destruction of Magdeburg, the excesses of the Imperialists in Lusatia, all combined to incense the Elector against the Emperor. The approach, too, of Gustavus Adolphus, (however slender his claims were to the protection of that prince,) tended to fortify his resolution. He accordingly forbade the quartering of the imperial soldiers in his territories, and announced his firm determination to persist in his warlike preparations. However surprised he should be, he added, "to see an imperial army on its march against his territories, when that army had enough to do in watching the operations of the King of Sweden, nevertheless he did not expect, instead of the promised and well merited rewards, to be repaid with ingratitude and the ruin of his country." To Tilly's deputies, who were entertained in a princely style, he gave a still plainer answer on the occasion. "Gentlemen," said he, "I perceive that the Saxon confectionery, which has been so long kept back, is at length to be set upon the table. But as it is usual to mix with it nuts and garnish of all kinds, take care of your teeth."

Tilly instantly broke up his camp, and, with the most frightful devastation, advanced upon Halle; from this place he renewed his demands on the Elector, in a tone still more urgent and threatening. The previous policy of this prince, both from his own inclination, and the persuasions of his corrupt ministers had been to promote the interests of the Emperor, even at the expense of his own sacred obligations, and but very little tact had hitherto kept him inactive. All this but renders more astonishing the infatuation of the Emperor or his ministers in abandoning, at so critical a moment, the policy they had hitherto adopted, and by extreme measures, incensing a prince so easily led. Was this the very object which Tilly had in view? Was it his purpose to convert an equivocal friend into an open enemy, and thus to relieve himself from the necessity of that indulgence in the treatment of this prince, which the secret instructions of the Emperor had hitherto imposed upon him? Or was it the Emperor's wish, by driving the Elector to open hostilities, to get quit of his obligations to him, and so cleverly to break off at once the difficulty of a reckoning? In either case, we must be equally surprised at the daring presumption of Tilly, who hesitated not, in presence of one formidable enemy, to provoke another; and at his negligence in permitting, without opposition, the union of the two.

The Saxon Elector, rendered desperate by the entrance of Tilly into his territories, threw himself, though not without a violent struggle, under the protection of Sweden.

Immediately after dismissing Tilly's first embassy, he had despatched his field-marshal Arnheim in all haste to the camp of Gustavus, to solicit the prompt assistance of that monarch whom he had so long neglected. The king concealed the inward satisfaction he felt at this long wished for result. "I am sorry for the Elector," said he, with dissembled coldness, to the ambassador; "had he heeded my repeated remonstrances, his country would never have seen the face of an enemy, and Magdeburg would not have fallen. Now, when necessity leaves him no alternative, he has recourse to my assistance. But tell him, that I cannot, for the sake of the Elector of Saxony, ruin my own cause, and that of my confederates. What pledge have I for the sincerity of a prince whose minister is in the pay of Austria, and who will abandon me as soon as the Emperor flatters him, and withdraws his troops from his frontiers? Tilly, it is true, has received a strong reinforcement; but this shall not prevent me from meeting him with confidence, as soon as I have covered my rear."

The Saxon minister could make no other reply to these reproaches, than that it was best to bury the past in oblivion.

He pressed the king to name the conditions, on which he would afford assistance to Saxony, and offered to guarantee their acceptance. "I require," said Gustavus, "that the Elector shall cede to me the fortress of Wittenberg, deliver to me his eldest sons as hostages, furnish my troops with three months' pay, and deliver up to me the traitors among his ministry."

"Not Wittenberg alone," said the Elector, when he received this answer, and hurried back his minister to the Swedish camp, "not Wittenberg alone, but Torgau, and all Saxony, shall be open to him; my whole family shall be his hostages, and if that is insufficient, I will place myself in his hands. Return and inform him I am ready to deliver to him any traitors he shall name, to furnish his army with the money he requires, and to venture my life and fortune in the good cause."

The king had only desired to test the sincerity of the Elector's new sentiments. Convinced of it, he now retracted these harsh demands. "The distrust," said he, "which was shown to myself when advancing to the relief of Magdeburg, had naturally excited mine; the Elector's present confidence demands a return. I am satisfied, provided he grants my army one month's pay, and even for this advance I hope to indemnify him."

Immediately upon the conclusion of the treaty, the king crossed the Elbe, and next day joined the Saxons. Instead of preventing this junction, Tilly had advanced against Leipzig, which he summoned to receive an imperial garrison. In hopes of speedy relief, Hans Von der Pforta, the commandant, made preparations for his defence, and laid the suburb towards Halle in ashes. But the ill condition of the fortifications made resistance vain, and on the second day the gates were opened. Tilly had fixed his head quarters in the house of a grave-digger, the only one still standing in the suburb of Halle: here he signed the capitulation, and here, too, he arranged his attack on the King of Sweden. Tilly grew pale at the representation of the death's head and cross bones, with which the proprietor had decorated his house; and, contrary to all expectation, Leipzig experienced moderate treatment.

Meanwhile, a council of war was held at Torgau, between the King of Sweden and the Elector of Saxony, at which the Elector of Brandenburg was also present. The resolution which should now be adopted, was to decide irrevocably the fate of Germany and the Protestant religion, the happiness of nations and the destiny of their princes. The anxiety of suspense which, before every decisive resolve, oppresses even the hearts of heroes, appeared now for a moment to overshadow the great mind of Gustavus Adolphus. "If we decide upon battle," said he, "the stake will be nothing less than a crown and two electorates. Fortune is changeable, and the inscrutable decrees of Heaven may, for our sins, give the victory to our enemies. My kingdom, it is true, even after the loss of my life and my army, would still have a hope left. Far removed from the scene of action, defended by a powerful fleet, a well-guarded frontier, and a warlike population, it would at least be safe from the worst consequences of a defeat. But what chances of escape are there for you, with an enemy so close at hand?" Gustavus Adolphus displayed the modest diffidence of a hero, whom an overweening belief of his own strength did not blind to the greatness of his danger; John George, the confidence of a weak man, who knows that he has a hero by his side. Impatient to rid his territories as soon as possible of the oppressive presence of two armies, he burned for a battle, in which he had no former laurels to lose. He was ready to march with his Saxons alone against Leipzig, and attack Tilly. At last Gustavus acceded to his opinion; and it was resolved that the attack should be made without delay, before the arrival of the reinforcements, which were on their way, under Altringer and Tiefenbach. The united Swedish and Saxon armies now crossed the Mulda, while the Elector returned homeward.

Early on the morning of the 7th September, 1631, the hostile armies came in sight of each other. Tilly, who, since he had neglected the opportunity of overpowering the Saxons before their union with the Swedes, was disposed to await the arrival of the reinforcements, had taken up a strong and advantageous position not far from Leipzig, where he expected he should be able to avoid the battle. But the impetuosity of Pappenheim obliged him, as soon as the enemy were in motion, to alter his plans, and to move to the left, in the direction of the hills which run from the village of Wahren towards Lindenthal. At the foot of these heights, his army was drawn up in a single line, and his artillery placed upon the heights behind, from which it could sweep the whole extensive plain of Breitenfeld. The Swedish and Saxon army advanced in two columns, having to pass the Lober near Podelwitz, in Tilly's front.

To defend the passage of this rivulet, Pappenheim advanced at the head of 2000 cuirassiers, though after great reluctance on the part of Tilly, and with express orders not to commence a battle. But, in disobedience to this command, Pappenheim attacked the vanguard of the Swedes, and after a brief struggle was driven to retreat. To check the progress of the enemy, he set fire to Podelwitz, which, however, did not prevent the two columns from advancing and forming in order of battle.

On the right, the Swedes drew up in a double line, the infantry in the centre, divided into such small battalions as could be easily and rapidly manoeuvred without breaking their order; the cavalry upon their wings, divided in the same manner into small squadrons, interspersed with bodies of musqueteers, so as both to give an appearance of greater numerical force, and to annoy the enemy's horse. Colonel Teufel commanded the centre, Gustavus Horn the left, while the right was led by the king in person, opposed to Count Pappenheim.

On the left, the Saxons formed at a considerable distance from the Swedes,— by the advice of Gustavus, which was justified by the event. The order of battle had been arranged between the Elector and his field-marshal, and the king was content with merely signifying his approval. He was anxious apparently to separate the Swedish prowess from that of the Saxons, and fortune did not confound them.

The enemy was drawn up under the heights towards the west, in one immense line, long enough to outflank the Swedish army,—the infantry being divided in large battalions, the cavalry in equally unwieldy squadrons. The artillery being on the heights behind, the range of its fire was over the heads of his men. From this position of his artillery, it was evident that Tilly's purpose was to await rather than to attack the enemy; since this arrangement rendered it impossible for him to do so without exposing his men to the fire of his own cannons. Tilly himself commanded the centre, Count Furstenberg the right wing, and Pappenheim the left. The united troops of the Emperor and the League on this day did not amount to 34,000 or 35,000 men; the Swedes and Saxons were about the same number. But had a million been confronted with a million it could only have rendered the action more bloody, certainly not more important and decisive. For this day Gustavus had crossed the Baltic, to court danger in a distant country, and expose his crown and life to the caprice of fortune. The two greatest generals of the time, both hitherto invincible, were now to be matched against each other in a contest which both had long avoided; and on this field of battle the hitherto untarnished laurels of one leader must droop for ever. The two parties in

Germany had beheld the approach of this day with fear and trembling; and the whole age awaited with deep anxiety its issue, and posterity was either to bless or deplore it for ever.

Tilly's usual intrepidity and resolution seemed to forsake him on this eventful day. He had formed no regular plan for giving battle to the King, and he displayed as little firmness in avoiding it. Contrary to his own judgment, Pappenheim had forced him to action. Doubts which he had never before felt, struggled in his bosom; gloomy forebodings clouded his ever-open brow; the shade of Magdeburg seemed to hover over him.

A cannonade of two hours commenced the battle; the wind, which was from the west, blew thick clouds of smoke and dust from the newly-ploughed and parched fields into the faces of the Swedes. This compelled the king insensibly to wheel northwards, and the rapidity with which this movement was executed left no time to the enemy to prevent it.

Tilly at last left his heights, and began the first attack upon the Swedes; but to avoid their hot fire, he filed off towards the right, and fell upon the Saxons with such impetuosity that their line was broken, and the whole army thrown into confusion. The Elector himself retired to Eilenburg, though a few regiments still maintained their ground upon the field, and by a bold stand saved the honour of Saxony. Scarcely had the confusion began ere the Croats commenced plundering, and messengers were despatched to Munich and Vienna with the news of the victory.

Pappenheim had thrown himself with the whole force of his cavalry upon the right wing of the Swedes, but without being able to make it waver. The king commanded here in person, and under him General Banner. Seven times did Pappenheim renew the attack, and seven times was he repulsed. He fled at last with great loss, and abandoned the field to his conqueror.

In the mean time, Tilly, having routed the remainder of the Saxons, attacked with his victorious troops the left wing of the Swedes. To this wing the king, as soon as he perceived that the Saxons were thrown into disorder, had, with a ready foresight, detached a reinforcement of three regiments to cover its flank, which the flight of the Saxons had left exposed. Gustavus Horn, who commanded here, showed the enemy's cuirassiers a spirited resistance, which the infantry, interspersed among the squadrons of horse, materially assisted. The enemy were already beginning to relax the vigour of their attack, when Gustavus Adolphus appeared to terminate the contest. The left wing of the Imperialists had been routed; and the king's division, having no longer any enemy to oppose, could now turn their arms wherever it would be to the most advantage. Wheeling, therefore, with his right wing and main body to the left, he attacked the heights on which the enemy's artillery was planted.

Gaining possession of them in a short time, he turned upon the enemy the full fire of their own cannon.

The play of artillery upon their flank, and the terrible onslaught of the Swedes in front, threw this hitherto invincible army into confusion. A sudden retreat was the only course left to Tilly, but even this was to be made through the midst of the enemy. The whole army was in disorder, with the exception of four regiments of veteran soldiers, who never as yet had fled from the field, and were resolved not to do so now. Closing their ranks, they broke through the thickest of the victorious army, and gained a small thicket, where they opposed a new front to the Swedes, and maintained their resistance till night, when their number was reduced to six hundred men. With them fled the wreck of Tilly's army, and the battle was decided.

Amid the dead and the wounded, Gustavus Adolphus threw himself on his knees; and the first joy of his victory gushed forth in fervent prayer. He ordered his cavalry to pursue the enemy as long as the darkness of the night would permit. The pealing of the alarm-bells set the inhabitants of all the neighbouring villages in motion, and utterly lost was the unhappy fugitive who fell into their hands. The king encamped with the rest of his army between the field of battle and Leipzig, as it was impossible to attack the town the same night. Seven thousand of the enemy were killed in the field, and more than 5,000 either wounded or taken prisoners. Their whole artillery and camp fell into the hands of the Swedes, and more than a hundred standards and colours were taken. Of the Saxons about 2,000 had fallen, while the loss of the Swedes did not exceed 700. The rout of the Imperialists was so complete, that Tilly, on his retreat to Halle and Halberstadt, could not rally above 600 men, or Pappenheim more than 1,400—so rapidly was this formidable army dispersed, which so lately was the terror of Italy and Germany.

Tilly himself owed his escape merely to chance. Exhausted by his wounds, he still refused to surrender to a Swedish captain of horse, who summoned him to yield; but who, when he was on the point of putting him to death, was himself stretched on the ground by a timely pistol-shot. But more grievous than danger or wounds was the pain of surviving his reputation, and of losing in a single day the fruits of a long life. All former victories were as nothing, since he had failed in gaining the one that should have crowned them all. Nothing remained of all his past exploits, but the general execration which had followed them. From this period, he never recovered his cheerfulness or his good fortune. Even his last consolation, the hope of revenge, was denied to him, by the express command of the Emperor not to risk a decisive battle.

The disgrace of this day is to be ascribed principally to three mistakes; his planting the cannon on the hills behind him, his afterwards abandoning these heights, and his allowing the enemy, without opposition, to form in order of battle. But how easily might those mistakes have been rectified, had it not been for the cool presence of mind and superior genius of his adversary!

Tilly fled from Halle to Halberstadt, where he scarcely allowed time for the cure of his wounds, before he hurried towards the Weser to recruit his force by the imperial garrisons in Lower Saxony.

The Elector of Saxony had not failed, after the danger was over, to appear in Gustavus's camp. The king thanked him for having advised a battle; and the Elector, charmed at his friendly reception, promised him, in the first transports of joy, the Roman crown. Gustavus set out next day for Merseburg, leaving the Elector to recover Leipzig. Five thousand Imperialists, who had collected together after the defeat, and whom he met on his march, were either cut in pieces or taken prisoners, of whom again the greater part entered into his service. Merseburg quickly surrendered; Halle was soon after taken, whither the Elector of Saxony, after making himself master of Leipzig, repaired to meet the king, and to concert their future plan of operations.

The victory was gained, but only a prudent use of it could render it decisive. The imperial armies were totally routed, Saxony free from the enemy, and Tilly had retired into Brunswick. To have followed him thither would have been to renew the war in Lower Saxony, which had scarcely recovered from the ravages of the last. It was therefore determined to carry the war into the enemy's country, which, open and defenceless as far as Vienna, invited attack. On their right, they might fall upon the territories of the Roman Catholic princes, or penetrate, on the left, into the hereditary dominions of Austria, and make the Emperor tremble in his palace. Both plans were resolved on; and the question that now remained was to assign its respective parts. Gustavus Adolphus, at the head of a victorious army, had little resistance to apprehend in his progress from Leipzig to Prague, Vienna, and Presburg. As to Bohemia, Moravia, Austria, and Hungary, they had been stripped of their defenders, while the oppressed Protestants in these countries were ripe for a revolt. Ferdinand was no longer secure in his capital: Vienna, on the first terror of surprise, would at once open its gates. The loss of his territories would deprive the enemy of the resources by which alone the war could be maintained; and Ferdinand would, in all probability, gladly accede, on the hardest conditions, to a peace which would remove a formidable enemy from the heart of his dominions. This bold plan of operations was flattering to a conqueror, and success perhaps might have justified it. But Gustavus Adolphus, as prudent as he was brave, and more a statesman than a conqueror, rejected it, because he had a higher end in view, and would not trust the issue either to bravery or good fortune alone.

By marching towards Bohemia, Franconia and the Upper Rhine would be left to the Elector of Saxony. But Tilly had already begun to recruit his shattered army from the garrisons in Lower Saxony, and was likely to be at the head of a formidable force upon the Weser, and to lose no time in marching against the enemy. To so experienced a general, it would not do to oppose an Arnheim, of whose military skill the battle of Leipzig had afforded but equivocal proof; and of what avail would be the rapid and brilliant career of the king in Bohemia and Austria, if Tilly should recover his superiority in the Empire, animating the courage of the Roman Catholics, and disarming, by a new series of victories, the allies and confederates of the king? What would he gain by expelling the Emperor from his hereditary dominions, if Tilly succeeded in conquering for that Emperor the rest of Germany? Could he hope to reduce the Emperor more than had been done, twelve years before, by the insurrection of Bohemia, which had failed to shake the firmness or exhaust the resources of that prince, and from which he had risen more formidable than ever?

Less brilliant, but more solid, were the advantages which he had to expect from an incursion into the territories of the League. In this quarter, his appearance in arms would be decisive. At this very conjuncture, the princes were assembled in a Diet at Frankfort, to deliberate upon the Edict of Restitution, where Ferdinand employed all his artful policy to persuade the intimidated Protestants to accede to a speedy and disadvantageous arrangement. The advance of their protector could alone encourage them to a bold resistance, and disappoint the Emperor's designs. Gustavus Adolphus hoped, by his presence, to unite the discontented princes, or by the terror of his arms to detach them from the Emperor's party. Here, in the centre of Germany, he could paralyse the nerves of the imperial power, which, without the aid of the League, must soon fall—here, in the neighbourhood of France, he could watch the movements of a suspicious ally; and however important to his secret views it was to cultivate the friendship of the Roman Catholic electors, he saw the necessity of making himself first of all master of their fate, in order to establish, by his magnanimous forbearance, a claim to their gratitude.

He accordingly chose the route to Franconia and the Rhine; and left the conquest of Bohemia to the Elector of Saxony.

Milton Keynes UK
Ingram Content Group UK Ltd.
UKHW031049120324
439302UK00006B/451